BUILD REAL WEALTH

BUILD REAL WEALTH

Practical Steps to Regain Financial Stability

SAM ADEYEMI

© Copyright 2012—Sam Adeyemi

All rights reserved. This book is protected under the copyright laws. This book may not be copied or reprinted for commercial gain or profit. The use of short quotations or occasional page copying for personal or group study is permitted and encouraged. Permission will be granted upon request. Unless otherwise identified, Scripture quotations are taken from the New King James Version. Copyright © 1982 by Thomas Nelson, Inc. Used by permission. All rights reserved. All emphasis within Scripture is the author's own.

Please note that Evangelista Media™ and Destiny Image™ Europe's publishing style capitalizes certain pronouns in Scripture that refer to the Father, Son, and Holy Spirit, and may differ from some Bible publishers' styles. Take note that the name satan and related names are not capitalized. We choose not to acknowledge him, even to the point of violating grammatical rules.

DESTINY IMAGE™ EUROPE srl
Via Maiella, 1
66020 San Giovanni Teatino (Ch) – Italy

"Changing the World, One Book at a Time."

This book and all other Evangelista Media™ and Destiny Image™ Europe books are available at Christian bookstores and distributors worldwide.

To order products, or for any other correspondence:

EVANGELISTA MEDIA™ Srl
Via della Scafa 29/14
65013 Città Sant'Angelo (Pe) – Italy
Tel. +39 085 4716623 • Fax: +39 085 9090113
Email: info@evangelistamedia.com
Or reach us on the Internet: www.evangelistamedia.com

ISBN 13: 978-88-96727-64-5
ISBN 13 EBOOK: 978-88-96727-66-9

For Worldwide Distribution, Printed in the U.S.A.
1 2 3 4 5 / 16 15 14 13 12

Contents

Chapter One	You Are Wealthy	7
Chapter Two	Redefining Wealth	25
Chapter Three	Money and Faith	45
Chapter Four	The Real Value of Your Mind	65
Chapter Five	The Spending Plan	89
Chapter Six	Breaking Free From Poverty	101
Chapter Seven	Starting a Business	121
Chapter Eight	Financial Freedom	143
	Endnotes	155

CHAPTER ONE

You Are Wealthy

One of the most fascinating stories I have read is told by Dr. Russell Conwell in his book *Acres of Diamonds*.[1] It is the story of a farmer who heard of a distant land where he could scoop loads of diamonds and become very rich. He sold his farm and set out for that distant land. He wandered about for years without finding such a land, became very broke, and eventually, out of frustration, jumped from a bridge and drowned. At about that time, the new owner of the farm discovered that the whole piece of land was sitting on acres of diamonds.

The lesson in the story, of course, is that our best opportunities can be found nearby. We only need to see them. But I would like to explore the implications of this story further. People can be rich without knowing and experiencing it. Being rich is something that runs deeper than acquiring cash. It emanates from the core of our belief system; that is, who we think we are. Being rich or being poor is a state of mind. The capacity to produce wealth rests entirely on the belief that we are wealthy.

So, let me ask—do you believe that you are rich, or do you believe that you are poor?

BATTLE OF IDENTITY

One of the greatest battles we will fight in life is the battle of identity. It is an internal battle. I fought this battle in the process of changing my inner reality from that of a poor person to that of a rich person. I needed to switch from believing that I was poor to believing that I am rich. You see, the impact of poverty goes beyond being deprived of basic material needs. It has psychological and emotional effects. And if a person stays long enough in deprivation, it becomes a spiritual problem to the extent that even when the person's physical circumstances have changed, the spiritual dimension to poverty can remain.

Take Israel for example, after the exodus from Egypt. It was easier for God to get them out of Egypt—than it was to get Egypt out of them. They had been conditioned by slavery to believe that they were poor and that they were victims. Eventually, God allowed a whole generation, less two people, to die in the wilderness[2] because they could not possess physically what they had not possessed in their hearts and minds. This is how Paul the apostle expressed this type of situation:

> *Therefore, since a promise remains of entering His rest, let us fear lest any of you seem to have come short of it. For indeed the gospel was preached to us as well as to them; but the word which they heard did not profit them, not being mixed with faith in those who heard it.*[3]

The problem was not with God's ability to bless them—it was with their own ability to conceptualize the thought of being prosperous, and being able to possess new territories as promised by God. Many who steal outrageous amounts of money do not realize that they are trying to use material things to cure a spiritual problem. It just doesn't work.

When you become rich in your heart, you will not be desperate anymore. You will have peace. You will have confidence. "For we who have believed do enter that rest...."[4] You will experience grace, and you will see God do in your life what you don't have the capacity to do. It has happened to me.

But again let me ask you—do you think you are rich or poor? Who you think you are either puts a limit on what you can do or opens you up to new opportunities.

You Have Won the Battle

There is good news for you and for me. We have won the battle over sin, poverty, and sickness. Jesus Christ's sacrifice won the battle on our behalf. Today we only have to enforce our victory when we believe that Jesus paid on the cross all that we owed satan and triumphed over him through Christ's resurrection. The following is one of the verses of Scripture that helped me win my internal battle over poverty:

> *For you know the grace of our Lord Jesus Christ, that though He was rich, yet for your sakes He became poor, that you through His poverty might become rich.*[5]

This is my simple understanding of the Scriptures; when Jesus paid for my sins, He also paid for my sicknesses and poverty. There were no sicknesses and poverty in the world until sin was introduced. Sin is the root; sicknesses and poverty are only fruit. The price that Christ paid for sin was the same payment He made for sicknesses and poverty.

He took my place as a sinner, now I can stand in His place in the presence of God as though I never committed even one sin. This is the greatest piece of information the human mind can grasp. It is truth that sets us free. "For He made Him who knew no sin to be sin for us, that we might become the righteousness of God in Him."[6]

Substitution has taken place. Christ took our place so we can take His place. We are free from hopelessness and powerlessness. We can take His place now as people who have right-standing with God. We can take His place as those who have power over sicknesses and diseases. Any disease that touches our bodies is trespassing on God's territory, and we can demand that it should leave us. Then we come to the issue of poverty. Our genetic coding has changed. We have the nature of God. We are not poor any longer. Christ took our place. He became poor so that we, through that poverty on the cross, can become rich.

I have accepted the offer. I am now rich. So I boldly declare, "I can never be poor again, the rest of my life." Of course, I know it is true only as long as I keep my part of the bargain, which is to obey God's instructions.

I hope the point is clear enough. If you are a believer, and you believe that you are a poor person who needs to struggle to become rich, you have been deceived. Don't struggle to become who you are already. Moreover, once you believe that you are poor, you will attract only poverty into your life. The job has been done on your behalf. Your part is to believe. "All things *are possible* to him who believes."[7] As a believer in Christ, you are not a poor person struggling to become rich. You are a rich person taking practical steps to convert your wealth to physical reality.

Enforce Your Victory

Wealth is first spiritual before it is physical. During the temptation of Jesus, it is recorded that the devil took Him to a very high mountain and showed Him all the kingdoms of the world, and the wealth and power of the world. Then he made a proposition to Jesus, "All these things I will give you if you will fall down and worship me."[8] It is helpful for us to be conscious of the fact that there are spiritual entities set over cities, nations, professions, and lines of business that try to control the flow of resources in these areas. We must subdue them and take possession of all God has provided for us to fulfill destiny. It is wise to remember, "When a strong man, fully armed, guards his own palace, his goods are in peace. But when a stronger than he comes upon him and overcomes him, he takes from him all his armor in which he trusted, and divides his spoils."[9]

Jesus refused satan's offer; there was no point going for the fake when He had access to the original. Satan can give you wealth and power, but because it is in his nature to lie, deceive, cheat, steal, kill, and destroy, if he ever gives you anything, you can be sure he will get it back several times over. Don't settle for the fake when you can get the original.

> *And you shall remember the Lord your God, for it is He who gives you power to get wealth, that He may establish His covenant which He swore to your fathers, as it is this day.* [10]

This power gives you the capacity to affect both the spiritual and physical realms in the process of wealth creation. God will not come down to take care of the devil on your behalf. He has given you the authority to put him where he belongs. "And these signs will follow those who believe: In My name they will cast out demons...."[11] Let this be a normal routine for you, that you break the power of the devil over the resources of your city and nation, and ask the angels of God to bring your possessions to you.

Accessing Spiritual Wealth

The resources that you get in the physical dimension will be the material equivalent of what you have received in the spiritual. Vision is the key to provision. Vision or revelation makes you a magnet that attracts the material equivalent of what you see in the vision. Or it gives you the ability to produce the physical equivalent of what is in the vision. We must maintain our access to revelation.

We access revelation through prayer. Prayer is a dialogue, not a monologue. We must be persistent in prayer until we know that revelation has been deposited in our hearts. "Call to Me, and I will answer you, and show you great and mighty things, which you do not know."[12] The point at which we receive revelation is the point at which we come into possession of what we desire spiritually. "Therefore I say to you, whatever things you ask when you pray, believe that you receive them, and you will have them."[13] This is our objective in this kind of prayer; to come to the point where we know that things have changed. Then when we say what God has said to us, the physical world must obey our voice. It is a cheaper way to make things work, especially with respect to our finances.

Another access to revelation is meditation. This is the art of thinking and pondering so that our hearts are ignited by insights. It just feels differently when it is God who has deposited a thought into your heart. Two disciples of Jesus who saw Him after His resurrection but did not recognize Him, said after He had revealed Himself and vanished, "Did not our heart burn within us while He talked with us on the road, and while He opened the Scriptures to us?"[14]

In the first Psalm, the blessed man is said to meditate in God's Word day and night. He is then likened to a tree planted by the rivers of water that bears fruit seasonally and whose leaf will never wither.[15] As water and nutrients cause fruits to come out of trees without groaning, so wealth and success show forth in the life of the one who receives ideas and spiritual power consistently from God. Find time to think. Use your imagination to connect with the invisible world using the Bible as your dream book. If you are too busy to think, you are too busy to prosper God's way.

We should also be open to prophetic instructions through God's messengers. When people speak under the inspiration of the Holy Spirit, what we get is not mere information. They are conduit pipes for the transfer of revelation into our hearts. In the Parable of the Sower, Jesus described revelation or divine ideas as seed, and the human heart as soil. One of the most strategic steps to take to change your status is to listen to or watch audio and video messages of ministers. Apart from the fact that you will get direct instructions to resolve specific issues, they will stir up your spirit to God's frequency to the extent that you will be able to download new visions and instructions from God. The Bible establishes a connection between prophets (by this I infer all of God's messengers) and our prosperity, "Believe in the Lord your God, and you shall be established; believe His prophets, and you shall prosper."[16]

Through giving, we can leverage on the law of exchange to receive revelations from God. I am aware that the message of giving has been abused and used to manipulate people to part with their money while promising them nothing short of magic. However, the presence of the fake is proof of the original. Abram gave Melchizedek a tenth of the spoils of war. Melchizedek (a manifestation of Christ in the Old Testament) gave him bread and wine, and blessed him.[17] What Abram gave was material, what he got in exchange was spiritual wealth that would continually produce material wealth in his life. Greed and revelation don't work together. "The generous soul will be made rich, and he who waters will also be watered himself."[18] When God asks us to give, it is not because He is desperately in need; it is to give Him the opportunity to release spiritual resources into our lives.

Take the case of Jacob as an example. He ran away from home because his brother Esau planned to kill him. He got to a place called Luz and passed the night using a stone for a pillow. He had a dream that night where he saw a ladder touching Heaven and earth, and saw angels ascending and descending on it. He renamed the place Bethel, which means the house of God. Then he made a vow to God, "If God will be with me, and keep me in this way that I am going, and give me bread to eat and clothing to put on, so that I come back to my father's house in peace, then the Lord shall be my God. And this stone which I have set as a pillar shall be God's house, and of all that You give me I will surely give a tenth to You."[19]

Jacob served his uncle for many years. Eventually, when it was time for him to leave, he had become a very wealthy man. And his wealth came from revelation. He explained to his two wives, that when their father fixed his wages to be spotted and speckled cattle, God caused all the plain-colored animals to give birth to spotted and speckled, offspring. An angel said to him in a dream of the night, "Lift your eyes now and see, all the rams which leap on the flocks are streaked, speckled and gray-spotted; for I have seen all that Laban is doing to you. I am the God of Bethel, where you anointed the pillar and where you made a vow to Me."[20] Jacob had access to revelation because of the vow he made to give to God. As a result, God interfered with the genetic coding of those animals. Jacob became more prosperous than his employer. Surely, giving gives access to spiritual wealth. And spiritual wealth attracts or produces its material equivalent in our lives.

It Gets Easier from Here

It is exciting when you attract or create wealth through the power of revelation. Take the case of Saul the son of Kish as an example from Scriptures. His father's donkeys went missing, so his father sent him and a servant to find them. Here is a description of their effort, "So he passed through the mountains of Ephraim and through the land of Shalisha, but they did not find them. Then they passed through the land of Shaalim, and they were not there. Then he passed through the land of the Benjamites, but they did not find them."[21]

When they got to the land of Zuph, Saul wanted them to return home, but the servant suggested they should meet Samuel the Prophet first. Something dramatic happened during Saul's meeting with the prophet. Samuel anointed Saul and told him that as soon as he left, he would meet two men who would tell him that the donkeys they had been looking for had been found.[22]

It seems to me that they ended their journey where they should have started it. Until Saul received spiritual impartation from Samuel, the donkeys avoided him. Miracles have a way of avoiding someone who has not received their spiritual equivalent. As soon as Saul's level of spiritual authority changed, the donkeys positioned themselves where they could be found.

Another case in point is that of Peter who confessed to Christ that he had toiled all night trying to catch fish and had caught nothing. But when he went back on the same sea after getting a revelation from Christ, fish swam into his net and almost pulled him overboard.[23]

Would you like to exercise mastery over the flow of resources—or would you prefer to deploy your own ability to struggle to acquire material help? Let God help you. It all begins with a simple prayer to establish a relationship with God by accepting His love and forgiveness through Jesus Christ. From here on, it gets a lot easier.

Now, how do you convert spiritual wealth into its material equivalent? That is what the rest of this book is about.

THE BASICS OF MONEY

I was posted to Lagos, Nigeria to pastor a branch church about two decades ago, and I came into the city with just a traveling bag hung on my shoulder. My first salary in the city was six hundred naira a month, and at the current exchange rate that is about four U.S. dollars (it was worth a bit more then). I came into the city with two suits, one of which I struggled so much to pay for as I needed it to be the best man at my friend's wedding. In fact, my friend eventually paid for it. It was sewed by a local tailor, but I couldn't wear it comfortably for church services because church members were wearing better ones. To cover my embarrassment, I would wear it going into the service; then after five minutes of praise and worship, I would take the jacket off, as though I was feeling very hot, and hang it on the chair. That was where it stayed for the remainder of the service.

However, my life has changed radically since then, and I believe that the insights that brought about the change, which are explored in this book, will change your life as well.

Wealth is spiritual in origin. Because the believer in Christ has access to spiritual resources, we are in good stead to have mastery over the flow of material and financial resources. God's original intention for us is to have dominion. There was never a moment of anxiety over financial or material provision in the ministry of Christ. His provision, in fact, went beyond the capacity of money. Obviously, He never entertained the thought of lack. He had abundance mentality. That is where we must begin from. John the beloved apostle wrote, "Beloved, I pray that you may prosper in all things and be in health, just as your soul prospers."[24] When we arrange the process of wealth creation in proper order, soul prosperity precedes material or financial prosperity. We must develop a wealth mentality based on revelation.

The fundamental difference between the poor and the rich is not in their bank accounts, it is in their hearts and minds. It is internal. The way rich people think is different from the way poor people think. When we change our thoughts, we change our lives. "And do not be conformed to this world, but be transformed by the renewing of your mind, that you may prove what is that good and acceptable and perfect will of God."[25] Those of us who belong to God's family should know how to work God's system in the very best possible way—not manipulating, but according to His will for us. We change our thinking by the power of revelation, and then our spiritual realities can become our physical realities.

With the global economic recession, many people are confused about their finances. The thing to do in a crisis is to go back to the basics. Circumstances may change, but principles never change. If you do not have a good grasp of the basics, you are likely to be the worst hit by the recession.

Let us consider the twenty pound note—the United Kingdom currency. On the side of the note that has the queen's picture is written, "Bank of England; I promise to pay the bearer on demand the sum of twenty pounds." It is signed by the chief cashier of the bank of England. The first time I read it I was confused. I thought, *You do not need to pay me anything, I have the twenty pounds already. Am I not holding twenty pounds?* The chief cashier says, "No, this is not the real twenty pounds; but if you present this, then we can give you the real thing." That is interesting, is it not?

I want to plead with you dear reader, please keep your mind open. You may be fighting a lot of mind battles as you go through this book. But bear in mind that being poor is a mindset and being rich is a mindset. So as you restructure your thinking, you will experience freedom. "You shall know the truth, and the truth shall make you free."[26]

Naaman went to Elisha the prophet to be healed of leprosy, and Elisha did not even come out of the house. He sent a message to the man and said, "Go wash at the river Jordan, seven times, and you will be healed." And the Scripture says that Naaman was angry. He said, "I thought the man would come out, look up to Heaven, call upon God, strike the place and heal the leper." He was furious; until somebody said to him, "Sir, if he had told you to do a more difficult thing, would you not have done it?"[27]

If I was there, I would have said to him, "General Naaman, calm down; it is not the prophet who has leprosy, it is you. It seems that you know how leprosy should be cured, in which case you should not have come here." Sometimes because of our prejudices, bias, and tradition, we hold on to ideas that frustrate our aspirations. Please keep your mind open. Real money is not paper; you do not see real wealth with your eyes. Let me explain further.

The Invention of Money

There was a time when people traded without money. They did trade by barter. If you grew tomatoes on your farm and I grew potatoes on mine, we met at the market and we exchanged them. We determined their relative values. This was determined by the amount of effort that was put into cultivating them and what it would take to replace them; that is the level of scarcity or demand for them. So I brought my potatoes, you brought your tomatoes, and we exchanged them. You went home with potatoes, I went home with tomatoes. That is how transactions were carried out.

If you wanted to pay the brick layer for building your house, you gave him potatoes or yam tubers; but of course with time, people realized it was difficult to carry out transactions like that. How do you pay for everything with yam tubers or with potatoes? When you wanted to pay your landlord at the end of the month, you gave him potatoes. If you wanted to pay your children's school fees, you took potatoes to the school. When you wanted to get on a bus, you gave potatoes to the driver. It was not easy. In fact sometimes, you came to the market with potatoes and the other person who came with tomatoes did not need your potatoes because he also grew potatoes on his farm. What do you do?

To make transactions easier, people invented money. Gold coins, silver coins, copper coins, and cowry shells represented the value of the potatoes at home. So if somebody had ten gold coins, it meant that he had produced something that had that value, and you could do business with the person. So the person who sold potatoes, therefore, took those gold coins or cowry shells and could use them to buy whatever he or she liked. Money makes transactions easier.

Real money is not the paper, it is the value the paper represents; and you cannot see value with your eyes. The paper and the coin represent value. I think it will make sense if we conclude that whoever came to the market then with nothing—no tomatoes, potatoes, clothes, shoes, rice, beans, nothing—would go home with no gold coins. Does that make sense? If you did not come to the market with a product, nobody would give you coins in exchange because you had nothing to exchange.

The material called money, paper or coin, is only a means of exchange. If you want to break free from poverty, keep this at the back of your mind. You will not get something for nothing. I know we can pray; I know we can bind the devil, crush his head, destroy all our enemies, put them inside coffins, and bury them spiritually. But when it comes to the issue of money, unless you bring something that has value, is usable, and will meet a need in somebody's life to the marketplace or the place of exchange, you will not receive money in exchange.

Without a product or service to offer, you may get a lot of money in the realm of the spirit, God may bless you with cars and houses in the spirit realm; but in this natural world, you may not have money because you have nothing to exchange. It makes sense, doesn't it? Real money is value.

And this impacts on ministry work, too. When Jesus gave His disciples the power to heal people, cure leprosy, cast out demons, and raise the dead, He told them not to bother to take money or extra clothes along. Because they were going to solve problems for people, they would receive money, food, and accommodation in exchange. The law of exchange is a powerful principle.

THE NEED TO DO BUSINESS

Several years ago, when our church was very young, we were not many then, and I really wanted to help our church members financially. But I discovered that all that I was teaching about finances was that they should give. One day I looked at my church members and thought to myself, *This people do not have the money, they cannot give what they do not have.* So I prayed, "Lord, is there anything in the Bible that can teach us how to get the money? I would rather teach the church members how to get the money first; and when they get it, then I can ask them to give it. As things are now, they do not have money. I do not have money either." And then the Holy Spirit took me on a journey—an experience that has been life-changing with powerful insights from the Bible.

One of the things I saw from the Bible, for example, is the need for people to start and run their own businesses. I am a crusader for entrepreneuring. God helped me to pull off my religious goggles, and I saw that Abraham was an entrepreneur,[28] Isaac was an entrepreneur,[29] and Jacob was an entrepreneur.[30] I said, "Oh my God, the God of Abraham, Isaac, and Jacob is a God of businessmen and women. He is a God of entrepreneurs."

If you do not think deeply, you will think that Abraham was a priest in a temple or synagogue. But Abraham, the father of faith, was actually a businessman. Maybe the one that blew my mind the most was the fact that Jesus was a businessman most of His life.[31] I know I just said something that sounds like blasphemy. But my emphasis is on the fact that as we began to teach church members how to start and run businesses, some of them said to me, "Well, the problem is capital. Where do we get capital? We do not have capital." So I decided to crack the capital issue from the Bible. And when I want to crack something, I always start from Genesis chapters 1 and 2; the two perfect chapters of the Bible.

You see, in Genesis chapters 1 and 2, there was no devil, no demon or sin. It was a perfect world. But from Genesis chapter 3, the devil showed up, and the rest of the Bible shows what God is doing to take humankind back to God's original intention. So I went to the creation story in Genesis and was looking for capital. The question on my mind was, *How much did God have when He wanted to create the world?* I read through the first two chapters of Genesis, but money was not mentioned there. So I said, if not having money is what makes a person poor, then at that time, God was broke. We all know He was not because He created the whole world anyway. So, that led me to a very powerful conclusion—it is not the absence of paper money that makes a person poor.

So what were the resources that God used to create our world? We get the answer from the Bible. "By faith we understand that the worlds were framed by the word of God, so that the things which are seen were not made of things which are visible."[32] That is interesting! I'll paraphrase it. The raw materials with which God created this physical world were invisible. The most powerful containers of value in our world are invisible. He used words to create our world.

REAL WEALTH IS INTANGIBLE

Words come from thoughts. "The earth was without form, and void; and darkness was on the face of the deep. ...Then God said, 'Let there be light.'"[33] In the natural, what you had was darkness. But God called out the light. This is because in His mind, He saw light. Not only that, He saw plants, animals, oceans, rivers, and mountains; that is where value and wealth creation begin. Thoughts have value.

Thoughts are powerful. Look around you, there is nothing that has value that did not begin first as a thought or idea in somebody's mind. Your vehicle, the faucets from which the water flows to have your bath or shower today, the design of your clothes; they all began as thoughts in people's minds. The basic raw material for creating things is thought. Wealthy people know that real wealth is intangible, and that when they get the intangible one, ultimately, they will get the tangible one.

This is where much of the developing world leaders and citizenry have a big problem—their definition of wealth is material. The only way they know a rich man is by the kind of car he drives. How will they know that "your money has arrived," like we say, if a person does not drive a Hummer? How will they know, if a person does not build a big house? How will they know that a breakthrough has arrived if people do not put on power suits and shirts or throw the biggest social parties in town?

Before God created man, He said, "Let Us make man in Our image, according to Our likeness; let them have dominion."[34] The same word that God spoke to the soil in which plants came out, the animals came out and oceans were created, were given to Adam and Eve to establish their wealth. He gave them the word, the revelation, as a resource to start with. And God blessed them and said, "Be fruitful and multiply; fill the earth and subdue it; have dominion."[35] That was what made them wealthy.

I can imagine that satan showed up and said something such as, "Eve, how will we know you are wealthy when you have nothing? We have to use something that is tangible, something you can touch and feel. You see that fruit—that is why it is important. God told you not to eat it because when you eat it, your eyes will be open, you will become like God."[36] It was a deception; Adam and Eve were wealthy already. They were like God already. They were created in the image of God!

One of the greatest lies the devil can tell to you is to make you believe that you are poor. Once you swallow it, you are hooked; you are in satan's net and the rest of your lifetime is spent struggling to get out of the net. Interestingly, after Adam and Eve ate the fruit, God drove them out of the Garden and that is when poverty started.

Jesus came to the river Jordan where He was baptized by John the Baptist. God spoke from Heaven, "This is My beloved Son, in whom I am well pleased."[37] Satan came and said something like, "There is no way for us to prove that You are powerful or wealthy. If You are the Son of God, turn this stone into bread." This was the same temptation he used on Adam and Eve. He wanted Jesus to define His power and wealth with material possessions. But

Jesus said, "It is written, 'Man shall not live by bread alone, but by every word that proceeds from the mouth of God.'"[38] In other words, He was not going to define His wealth by the material; He was going to define it with the intangible.

Jesus said, "Therefore do not worry, saying, 'What shall we eat?' or 'What shall we drink?' or 'What shall we wear?'" That describes the tangible. Then He said, "Seek first the kingdom of God and His righteousness," which describes the intangible—"and all these things shall be added to you."[39]

When you define wealth only by the material, you are likely to be deceived. Anytime you do not have cash, your sense of security will be threatened; you will feel poor. That is the foundation for corruption. If you do not have real value, I mean the intangible one, even if you acquire millions of dollars through fraudulent means, you are still poor. And if you read the Bible very well, you will realize that if you go down that road like it happened for Adam and Eve, you will attract a curse that will eventually wipe out all the material things that you accumulated.

I tell people that I can never be poor again for the rest of my life, and it has nothing to do with the money in my bank account. It has to do with the intangible resources available to me. God's Word says, "And the Word became flesh...."[40] In other words the invisible became visible; the intangible became tangible. Once you get spiritual wealth, it is just a matter of time before it attracts its material equivalent into your life. Therefore, if someone steals the material one, he cannot impoverish you. Your intangible wealth will reproduce its material equivalent again.

CHAPTER TWO

Redefining Wealth

I heard this story many years ago. A man was coming from the area where a crusade had just been held, and on the way he met armed robbers. They pointed a gun at him and said, "Your money or your life!" He said, "I'm sorry, I don't have either. I'm just coming from a crusade. They asked us to give an offering there, and I gave all the money on me. At the end of the service, the evangelist asked who wanted to give their lives to Christ, and I gave my life to Christ—so I don't have money and I don't have my life." We can only imagine that the robbers were left scratching their heads.

Now let's move on to defining, or redefining, wealth. When we understand what wealth is, we define wealth more by the intangible than by the tangible. That is where many have missed it, because they have been trying to build wealth on the wrong foundation. Unfortunately, this is especially true of the understanding of wealth in much of the developing world. It is a cultural problem. Our definition of wealth is largely material. We do not believe that a person is wealthy until the person has a big house, loads of cash, expensive cars, expensive clothes and jewelry, and throws big parties. Because of our lack of value for intangible wealth, we have missed out on the greater part of the wealth that God has given us as a continent, as a nation, and of course as individuals. Endowed with an unusual measure of natural resources, many developing nations are still struggling to break out of the cycle of poverty.

I want to emphasize that intangible resources are powerful, and you cannot call someone who has those intangible resources poor. If you call yourself poor because you do not have money in the bank, you are the one who is impoverishing yourself. "For as he thinks in his heart, so is he."[1] If a person thinks he is poor, then that person is poor no matter how favorable his circumstances may be.

We need to pay attention to those intangible resources at our disposal. Earlier on I asked the question, how much did God have when He was creating the world? What resources did He use in creating the world? He had nothing but His thoughts and then He spoke His word. Thoughts are powerful resources. If you know that, you do not joke with your capacity to think. One of the greatest investments you can make in this life is to invest in your ability to think. This is because to a large extent, the greatest resources you will use to create your wealth will come in the form of thoughts.

There are countries that value ideas as intellectual property. Why? They discovered that ideas have as much value as tangible things such as land, homes, and cars, if not more. Whereas people receive ownership certificates or deeds for land, some countries have defined laws on intellectual property that confer on individuals the ownership of their ideas. If it is your original idea, it is your intellectual property. So you can sell, lease, or rent an idea the way you do a piece of land.

Turning Intangible Wealth into Cash

One of the wealthiest men in the world is Bill Gates.[2] He is wealthy not only because of material wealth but because of intellectual property. The world has redefined wealth and many countries have been left behind. Some young, enterprising people have set up Websites and within one or two years, they were multibillionaires because of the ideas they presented on their Websites. How familiar are you with the Internet? It's a virtual world—no walls, floors, ceilings, yet business is being conducted and fortunes are being made. The world has tapped into the realm of the invisible—where real wealth is.

You will observe, therefore, that in countries where value is placed on thoughts they also value plans. This is because plans are the products of thoughts. They value the future because the future is created in our thoughts. They value dreams; they talk about their national dreams and the dreams of their leaders. "The *plans* of the diligent lead surely to plenty."[3] That is Solomon speaking, and if Solomon talks about plenty, he sure knows what he is talking about. If you check the major differences between wealthy people and poor people, you will see that the average wealthy person has plans and goals that are written down. The average poor person does not have a plan.

If ideas are powerful and have value, if they are intellectual property, then the equipment that produces the ideas must be valuable—the human mind. The greatest mining field of the world is the human mind. Whereas the wealthiest people in the world were those who owned gold or diamond deposits, now the wealthiest people in the world are those who have intellectual property, who dig gold from their minds.

The human mind is powerful. It has the capacity to design, invent, and innovate. So, your wealth is tied to the use of your mind. It should be obvious that the people who move the greatest amount of money around are usually people who sit in air-conditioned offices and move things with their pens or by typing on the computer keyboard. It is not always the people who sweat the most; it is those who think the most. Thinking gives value to the sweat. If we realize this, then we should invest in our thinking.

I have observed that many who sweat while praying for money have not invested in their capacity to think. I have seen people try to substitute such intense activity in prayer for the development of the mind, and I wish we would wake up and realize that our lives will be transformed by the renewing of our minds. We must find the connection between our prayers and the quality of our thoughts. If we want to pray, we must pray first for a change in our thinking.

And this is where the believer has a great advantage. We have access to the spirit of wisdom who can take our thinking into God's dimension. "But as it is written: 'Eye has not seen, nor ear heard, nor have entered into the heart of man, the things which God has prepared for those who love Him.' But God has revealed them to us through His Spirit. For the Spirit searches all things, yes, the deep things of God."[4] When we think like God, we can create wealth out of impossible situations, and we experience miracles of supernatural provision.

TIME AS A RESOURCE

Time is a resource. The wealthy part of the world values time. Who invented African time? That person had poverty mentality. He was trying to justify the lack of value that we attach to time. When business people say, "Time is money," they mean time is a convertible resource. Time can be converted to love if you would sit down and have an intimate discussion with someone and show the person attention and affection. Time can also be converted to money, and there is no way you will develop the capacity to turn it into money if you cannot measure its rate. So when people discovered the connection between time and money, they invented the clock. Because if you can measure the rate at which time passes, then you will be able to determine the rate at which you make money with time.

How do you convert time to money?

Convert Time to Wisdom

Converting time to wisdom means that you can convert time into the development of your thinking ability; that is what you do when you go to school. A student goes into the university for some years, graduates, and is called a doctor. That student has converted those years into the ability to cure people of illnesses and diseases. And because of that ability, which is essentially centered in the mind, the person now has a right to earn money because the person can give out value in terms of curing sicknesses and diseases. So you convert time to wisdom and skill, then the skill brings the money.

Value Time over Money

Time is valuable. Poor people value money over time. They spend time trying to conserve money. Rich people spend money trying to conserve time. Example: two people want to travel from one city to another for business. The roundtrip airfare is about $200; driving would cost about $80. One person looks at the money at his disposal and says, "Two hundred dollars?" He says, "Even if I have the money for airfare, I am not going to spend it." So he starts driving—the distance takes him about twelve hours. Another person goes to the airport, boards a plane, and in forty-five minutes arrives in the destination city. She quickly does whatever she has to do in about two to three hours, and in another forty-five minutes she is back in her home office. The person who is trying to save money is still on the road driving to the city.

But you may say, "But what if I do not have the money?" Oh, that is okay. It is understandable if you cannot access the cash at this point, but in your thinking, do not justify it. Just tell yourself, *Someday when I do have the money, I am going to travel the most efficient way, because that will be a better use of my time. There is coming a time when I am going to make the best use of my time.*

At the right time, I want to initiate a labor policy in my country, Nigeria, to pay people per hour. (I know it is the practice already in many countries.) This compels people to make a connection between their time and their money. Presently, because many have not made that connection, we waste much time. It could restructure our economy completely if we paid people per hour. Then all the frequent excuses to attend naming ceremonies, funerals, or wedding ceremonies during office hours—with their salary still complete at the end of the month—will change. And some realize that it is oftentimes wise to send a financial gift to someone celebrating rather than taking time away from the office to attend. And hopefully entertaining guests during office hours will cease.

People are paid to produce value in exchange for the money they receive. When a friend who has nothing to do comes by and takes one hour of an office worker's time, that worker just gave their boss's money away.

I ask you to please write down your monthly income. Now write down the number of hours that you work per month and divide your income by the number of hours that you work per month. This shows you what one hour of your time is currently worth. You can determine from that number whether to invest or spend your time, and at what rate.

Many people frequently make demands on my time. While that is okay, I see that some do not realize that when they take my time, they take one of my most valuable resources. If I give you a car, I can buy another one; but if I give you one hour of my time, I can never recover it. Once it is gone, it is gone forever; time is a resource that can never be replaced once it is expended. So when you waste your time, you are not just wasting your time, you are wasting your money and your life. Dr. Myles

Munroe[5] says that some people say they are just trying to kill time because they do not have anything to do. Dr. Munroe says killing time is not murder, it is suicide.

Time is a resource. I am hoping that you will realize that once you start thinking this way, you will be surprised how wealthy you are. You may have been broke or poor because you thought you were poor, but you are not. You are too blessed to be poor!

When talking about time, do you know the most exciting thing about it? Almighty God has given to all human beings, irrespective of their status, the same amount of time. Wow! Is that not fair enough? So, what are you going to do with it?

VALUES ARE INTANGIBLE WEALTH

All people have values; they are principles or qualities that we have adopted as our personal standards. Some people value love, some value recreation. Others value financial independence. These examples show the personal standard each individual has adopted. We can convert values to income through honesty, valuing people, and valuing the intangible. Here's what I mean:

Honesty

Many people do not realize that honesty as a personal standard is wealth. It is intangible wealth that ultimately can be converted into cash. If you have a million dollars, and two people come to you with similar business proposals, each of them needing start-up capital of half a million dollars with a promise to pay back your money in six months with 20 percent interest on your money, what will determine your willingness to invest your money? Their integrity! It will be their ability to keep their promises. The less you trust a person, the less likely your money flows to that person. This means that honesty or integrity is something that can be taken to the place of exchange the way people carry potatoes and tomatoes to the market. Someone can take honesty to the market and go back home with money. When people understand this, they will not destroy their character and reputation to make quick money. The less integrity you have, the poorer you are. "A good name is to be chosen rather than great riches, loving favor rather than silver and gold."[6]

Where there is honesty, there is trust. In the economic world, trust is called social capital. So when there is trust, you can carry out transactions. I can sell my goods without getting cash in return because the person who is buying my goods has promised to bring my cash. The collateral that the person uses is his or her honesty. When there is trust in the place of financial transactions, it increases the velocity of money. The velocity of money is the rate at which money travels. When there is a high velocity, then you can make a lot of money with little investment.

Imagine that someone buys a product for ten dollars and sells it for fifteen dollars. And he is able to sell ten pieces a day. But he has only ten dollars to invest. So he buys one, sells it, goes back, buys another, sells it, buys one again and sells it. Of course with time, he can then buy two or three at a time. But the point is, if he does that for ten days, he will make a lot of money. On the other hand, his friend can invest $500 to buy fifty pieces but sell only one piece in a week. A $500 investment compared to a ten dollar investment, and yet the person with the ten dollar investment makes more money. That is what velocity of money does; it multiplies the rate at which we create wealth.

Now when there is honesty and trust, the velocity of money increases because people transact business more quickly. When there is no trust, it slows down the velocity of money like we have now in my country. Because of lack of trust, we carry out most of our transactions with cash. It is slowing us down; the world has left that point. They use credit cards or checks because real money is not the paper. It is value, and you can represent that value in different ways. There are parts of the world where you can walk into a shop and pay for goods with a check; that makes it easier, does it not? So even if you do not have cash but you have your check book, you can pay with your check and go with the clothes, groceries, whatever you need. But when trust is eroded in a society, all of us become poor for it. Your integrity is money.

Value People

The ultimate resource on this planet is human life. Wealthy countries put value on people. I see an absurdity in many developing countries; I see people who value money over human beings. That is why people carry out ritual killings in Africa. The person who kills another human being in order to make a charm that will produce money is a fool. He will never be truly rich. In fact, when I read our newspapers, I see that most of the people who do those things are wretched.

If we value human beings, our social services will change. In fact, everything will change. If there is value for human life, we understand the reason for standards—in workplace safety, carbon emission levels, homeland security, etc. When we value human life, we understand why hospitals are important and why they should be properly equipped. There is no amount of money or effort that is too much to expend on one life. Jesus said, "What profit is it to a man if he gains the whole world, and loses his own soul? Or what will a man give in exchange for his soul?"[7] In His estimation, one human soul is greater than the whole material world put together.

In some countries, a rich man's car can have more value than the life of a human being. We cannot build a wealthy nation on people who have a low sense of their self-worth. We must *develop* people. It is through the use of the human mind that we realize the greatest potential of material resources. You can have gold, silver, iron ore, and timber, you can have oranges, animals, or anything, but it is when you bring in the use of the mind that the best value, the intrinsic value in each resource can be powerfully realized. Whatever you do, put your greatest premium on people, and you will prosper. Treat people like kings and queens, and be willing to go to any length to serve them. You *will* succeed.

Value the Intangible

People who value intangible resources will always be more prosperous than those who value material resources alone. I have an illustration from the Bible; two brothers, twins, Esau and Jacob went into a transaction. I want you to see what they traded by barter:

> *Now Jacob cooked a stew; and Esau came in from the field, and he was weary. And Esau said to Jacob, "Please feed me with that same red stew, for I am weary." Therefore his name was called Edom. But Jacob said, "Sell me your birthright as of this day." And Esau said, "Look, I am about to die; so what is this birthright to me?" Then Jacob said, "Swear to me as of this day." So he swore to him, and sold his birthright to Jacob. And Jacob gave Esau bread and stew of lentils; then he ate and drank, arose, and went his way. Thus Esau despised his birthright.*[8]

Esau despised the intangible. I do not know if you have thought deeply before about this transaction. Somebody has food and the other one comes in and says, "I want this food." The one with the food is a thinker. He is smart. He says, "Oh no, you do not get something for nothing." That is life, is it not? For anyone to think that he will get money without bringing anything that has value, no product or service that will meet a need is an exercise in self-deception. It does not work that way.

So Jacob says, "Mister, you cannot get the food for free. There is going to be an exchange. This food has value; it cost me something to prepare it." And then he says, "Let me suggest to you what you should sell. When I give you the food, you give me your birthright." Let me ask; what is a birthright? Has anyone seen it before? The birthright was the right to inherit their father's property when he died. And that right went naturally to the first son. Though they were twins, Esau came out first. So he was going to get the greater part of their father's goods someday in the future when the father died. The man was not dead yet. So the birthright was intangible. It was a future promise.

Jacob valued the future promise, something that he could not hold yet, more than the tangible. Esau valued the visible more than the invisible; he valued the present more than the future. So the transaction happened and they went their way. And Esau was happy. He got the food, and Jacob seemed to get nothing. Then one day, when the future arrived, their father Isaac said, "I am about to go," and he called Esau because he was not aware of the transaction.

But we cannot break God's laws. The laws that control the universe cannot be broken; we can only break ourselves against the law. So the law kicked in; what a man sows that he shall reap. And the mother, because she favored Jacob more, quickly hinted to him. "Your father wants to release a blessing; he sent your brother out to get food. You go ahead, prepare the meat, give it to your father, and take the blessing."[9]

For a long time they taught us in church that Jacob was a crooked fellow, and a cheat. But who really was the cheat in this transaction? Was it not the person who took the porridge and still wanted to take the birthright?

I am making a point; the people who value the intangible, who value visions, dreams, knowledge, ideas, plans, time, ultimately will be more prosperous than those who value only material resources. And that is so visible in our world today. Japan has almost nothing in terms of natural resources, and yet it has one of the most powerful economies in the world. It takes raw materials from countries that have them, adds ideas, and produces things in mass quantities. It produces cars, electronics, and diverse products and sells them—consequently, Japan is one of the wealthiest countries in the world. No wonder Jesus said, "Do not worry, saying, 'What shall we eat?' or 'What shall we drink?' or 'What shall we wear?'" Those are material things, are they not? He said, "Seek first the kingdom of God and His righteousness, and all these things shall be added to you."[10] If you have the intangible, the tangible is coming.

Jesus said something else about worldly treasures and material possessions:

> *Do not lay up for yourselves treasures on earth, where moth and rust destroy and where thieves break in and steal; but lay up for yourselves treasures in heaven, where neither moth nor rust destroys and where thieves do not break in and steal.*[11]

What was he saying? Build more intangible wealth than tangible. If all your wealth is only tangible, and someone steals it, you are in trouble. If your wealth is intangible in the first place, nobody can steal the intangible. As long as you have intangible wealth, the principle will always kick in for you. If you get intangible resources from God, you will be more prosperous than the people around who have tangible resources. You will rise beyond your contemporaries. Whatever is limiting people will not be able to limit you. If you align with the principles of God, His blessings will come upon you and overtake you.

If you build your self-esteem or your sense of identity on material things, your success will not last. You will find it difficult to win over temptation like Jesus did. Satan told Him, "If You are the Son of God, command that these stones become bread."[12] In other words, produce tangible results and prove your value. You will do desperate things if you define your value by the material.

The devil then took Jesus to the tip of the temple and told Him, "If You are the Son of God, throw Yourself down."[13] It sounds like, "Show Your power. Do something spectacular, the kind that nobody has ever seen before." Then the devil took Jesus to a very high mountain, showed Him all the kingdoms of the world in a moment, and their glory. Satan said, "All these things I will give You if You will fall down and worship me."[14] Why was the devil asking for the intangible in exchange for the tangible? Jesus did not have the spirit of Esau; He refused. There are Esau nations and there are Jacob nations. There are Esau families and Jacob families. There are still Esaus and Jacobs in our world today. The good news is that you can change your character by changing your thinking. You can change your value system. Eventually, you know what Esau did? He cried. I pray in the name of Jesus that you will not make wrong choices that will lead to regrets.

I love the transaction between Abraham and Melchizedek. Abraham had just conquered the armies of three countries combined and he was coming back with the spoils of war. God's Word says, "Then Melchizedek king of Salem brought out bread and wine; he was the priest of God Most High. And he blessed him and said, 'Blessed be Abraham of God Most High, possessor of heaven and earth; and blessed be God Most High, who has delivered your enemies into your hand.'"[15] That was what Melchizedek told him. How many people have seen the blessing with their eyes before? It is intangible. It is invisible. But it eventually produces its material equivalent in your life.

Melchizedek blessed Abraham, and the Bible says Abraham gave him the tithe of all. So when God says, "Bring your tithes and offerings and I will pour you out a blessing that you won't have enough room to take,"[16] He wants to give you intangible wealth. He wants to give you ideas—the power of blessing and favor—the thing that causes people to see you, to love you, to prefer you and to want to help you. He wants to open up avenues for you to acquire skill more than before.

God's Word says, "Now the king of Sodom said to Abram, 'Give me the persons, and take the goods for yourself.' But Abram, said to the king of Sodom, 'I have raised my hand to the Lord, God Most High, the Possessor of heaven and earth, that I will take nothing from a thread to a sandal strap, and that I will not take anything that is yours, lest you should say, 'I have made Abram rich.'"[17] Ah! Do not beg. When you have spiritual wealth, nobody can intimidate you with material wealth. When you have the intangible and you value it and you know how rich and how wealthy you are, you will not permit yourself to believe you are poor or broke to the point where you turn somebody else into your source of provision.

Abraham could have taken everything. He was the one who fought the war; he could have taken all that material wealth, but he said, "No, I don't need it, I have wealth. If I take this away from you now, I would have created the opportunity for you to claim tomorrow that you are the one who made me rich." This is how it should be. Don't go around begging; it is an insult to your position as a child of the living God.

Developing Prosperity Consciousness

This is where I am really going with this; you must develop a prosperity consciousness. You must come to the point where you know that you are rich. See yourself as being rich; think like you are rich. Nobody legitimately acquires wealth in our world without a prosperity consciousness, knowing deep within that they are rich and prosperous.

I used to think that the day I would get a lot of money, I would become rich; but God delivered me. I became rich even when I did not have money. And then I discovered that the money did not have a choice than to find its way into my account. There is nothing on this earth that will not obey God's voice, because everything was created by the Word. It was not when millions entered my account that I became a millionaire. When I became a millionaire, the millions had no option but to find their way into my bank account. It is first within, and then without.

The following are tips for developing a prosperity consciousness:

1. Believe what the Word of God says about you. You may have been born into a poor family. Maybe you could not get all the education you wanted. That is what happened. But who are you now? Will you allow your circumstances and experiences to define you, or will you allow God to define who you are? "For you know the grace of our Lord Jesus Christ, that though He was rich, yet for your sakes He became poor, that you through His poverty *might* become rich."[18] He was rich, we were poor. On the cross, the work of substitution happened; He took our place as sinners, so we could take His place as the righteous one in God's presence. Poverty came into our world as a result of sin. As mentioned previously, the price that He paid for sin was the price that He paid for sicknesses, diseases, and poverty. Notice it is the word "might." Your choice is involved. So if He became poor on the cross, why should you still be poor? He took the poverty, what do you have left? Prosperity! You are rich!

And God will not only look at what you have materially to define your wealth because He does not only see the material, He sees the invisible also. If God says you are rich, you are rich. Anybody who preaches to you and tells you that as a child of God you are a poor person who needs to struggle and battle the devil to become rich, that person has deceived you.

When Jesus hung on that cross, He had no business hanging on the cross—He hung on that cross on your behalf. In the eyes of God the Father, you were the one hanging there. Every price for every sin you ever committed or will commit was paid there. You do not owe the devil a dime anymore, everything was paid. "I have been crucified with Christ; it is no longer I who live, but Christ [who can never be broke, who can never be poor] lives in me."[19] You are not a poor person struggling to become rich—you are a rich person taking practical steps now and adjusting your thinking to manifest your wealth.

Who are you? Ask yourself that question again. Rich or poor, who are you? We have come to the place of warfare, because there are battles raging in our minds right now. How can I call myself rich when I don't have money? That is what we are talking about. You are not what you wear, you are not what you have; you are who God says you are. Until you have "thought money," you are not likely to have paper money.

Peter and John came across the lame man at the gate called Beautiful. The man looked at them expectantly hoping they would give him money. Peter said, "Silver and gold have I none; but such as I have...."[20] You know, for some people, it is silver and gold I have none, full stop. Once they do not have silver and gold, naira, pound sterling, dollars, a car, or a house, they are finished. They have no value. But although you may not have silver and gold now, you still have something. The something that you have will produce the silver and the gold. The silver and the gold know where they should go. They look for their spiritual equivalent. If silver and gold is in the hand of someone who does not have spiritual wealth, it is only there temporarily.

"Eye has not seen, nor ear heard, nor have entered into the heart of man the things which God has prepared for those who love Him."[21] You cannot have the Spirit of the living God in your heart and become poor. People who call you poor make a big mistake, and there is no point arguing with them. Very soon, they will discover the truth. There is a reason why I tell people I can never be poor again the rest of my life. I have found the real thing, and I'm not referring to the national or global economy. I am connected to another economy; it is a superior economy. I have access to gold that is better than the material gold that you can handle. To access our wealth, we must have a revelation of the finished work of Christ on the cross.

2. Get an idea or revelation from God. For each situation in your life, get an idea or revelation from God. Peter and his friends who were fishing could not catch fish all through the night. But then they got one instruction from Jesus and fish swam right into the nets.[22] When God gives you an idea, He is giving you wealth.

3. Watch your associations. The people who are close to you either give you thoughts of wealth or thoughts of poverty. The unfortunate thing for the average poor person is that their best friends are also poor. And when I say poor, I mean people who have a poverty mindset—people who do not have intangible wealth. I can never despise the person who does not have a pair of shoes but who has self-esteem. I cannot despise such a person because I know it is just a matter of time that the person's word will become flesh. That person's dream will attract its material equivalent. His or her vision will attract provision. It is a law. I am talking about the person who "thinks broke." The Bible says, "He who walks with wise men will be wise, but the companions of fools will be destroyed."[23]

Look at the blessed man in the Psalms:

> *Blessed is the man who walks not in the counsel of the ungodly, nor stands in the path of sinners, nor sits in the seat of the scornful; but his delight is in the law of the LORD, and in His law he meditates day and night. He shall be like a tree planted by the rivers of water; that brings forth its fruit in its season, whose leaf also shall not wither; and whatever he does shall prosper.*[24]

In your leisure time, write the names of the seven people who are closest to you. If you are married, your spouse is first, if you have children, write children so they take only one space. Fill the remaining five spaces. When you are done with that, please take a good look at the list; you are looking at your future. The quality of your life will likely not be better than those of the people on that list. The point is that the people who influence your thoughts most, influence your financial well-being. If you change one name on that list, you can change your financial status.

4. Get a mentor; a financial mentor. Hang around someone who is already producing the kind of results you want. I have heard that some people believe that some of my mentors have given me a lot of money. Unfortunately, they got it wrong. Well, they have given me money, but not the kind that people think. They have given me ideas, dreams, and vision about myself. They have given me wisdom. In other words, they have given me intangible wealth, which in turn has produced visible wealth.

Abraham gave Isaac both material and intangible wealth—the blessing. Famine wiped out the tangible one, but it could not wipe out the intangible one. The intangible one produced a fresh round of tangible wealth even in the midst of famine.[25]

Your mentor is a picture of your future. When I look at my mentors, I say to myself, *if they can do it, I also can do it.* That breaks limits in my mind. Then the limits come off in the flow of material resources to me. If what you think you should do with your mentor is to take money from him or her, you are making a big mistake. That is not the purpose of a mentor. The wisdom of your mentor is more valuable to you than his or her material wealth. It is intangible wealth that makes you a magnet for material wealth.

5. Read books. Several years ago, I was walking by a bookshop in an airport hotel, and I stopped and decided to walk in. This must have been maybe some thirteen years or so ago. I saw the book, *Think and Grow Rich* by Napoleon Hill.[26] I bought it. That is one of the best investments I ever made in my life. This is because the thoughts, ideas, and the insights poured into my mind from Napoleon Hill's book, and they gave me wealth. I got it. I cannot even quantify the amount of wealth Napoleon Hill gave me through his book which I bought for the equivalent of three dollars.

In Napoleon Hill's book I read that thoughts are things, tangible things, and that I should learn to give value to thoughts. And I read in the book how to organize those thoughts and act on them till they produce their material equivalent. It is not every part of the book I agree with, but I will tell you that there are powerful principles there; and as I read each line, Scriptures came to me because of my familiarity with the Bible. This is how I got money from wealthy people; by reading their books. Also, I have made a commitment, seeing how it works, to give wealth to others. But many people to whom I am giving wealth do not recognize where I have hidden the money. And they would not believe that I have given them anything until I give them cash. I give people a lot of cash, but the people who get the greatest wealth from me are the ones who get ideas, thoughts, concepts, and spiritual wealth.

6. Get educated. Anyone who deprives you of the ability to get education steals your money. You may not realize it now, but you will realize it in the future—like Esau. It is like the stealing of a birthright. Education is the process through which you empower the mind to create solutions to problems. You get money in exchange for the problems you solve. If you cannot get formal education, educate yourself. Read books. Listen to audio programs. Watch educational programs on video. Attend seminars or short-term courses. Serve an apprenticeship. Whatever you do, invest in your ability to think.

Let me pray for you. I see the heavens open over you. I see the Spirit of God resting on you like He rested on Jesus.[27] Revelation and spiritual power will be made available to you continuously. I see you gain access to dimensions of wealth that nobody in your country has ever accessed before. I declare you are not poor; you are rich. I declare that the curse of poverty that satan has placed over families and nations will have no effect over your life. As Melchizedek blessed Abraham, I bless you. God said to Abraham, "…blessing I will bless you, and multiplying I will multiply your descendants."[28] I prophesy that the thing—the blessing—that turns a human being into a magnet rests on your life from today forward. Any wrong definition of who you are, what you have, and what you can do, that was ever embedded into your mind and heart is destroyed in the name of Jesus Christ.

Chapter Three

Money and Faith

You must change your belief system if you want to experience material wealth. One major characteristic of people who are prosperous in our world is that they *think* they are prosperous. This is very important. The way the human spirit is designed, it operates by the force of faith. When the human heart believes or accepts something as reality, there is power that goes forth from it to organize circumstances and to influence the material world to agree or to align with that reality. That is why Jesus said, "whoever says to this mountain, 'Be removed and be cast into the sea,' and does not doubt in his heart, but believes that those things he says will be done, he will have whatever he says."[1]

The force of the human spirit is unleashed through faith. All things are possible to them who believe. Two blind men met Jesus and said, "Have mercy on us." He said to them, "According to your faith be it unto you."[2] Those two men believed their eyes would open—and instantly their eyes were opened. If you understand that, then your greatest quest should be to get your heart to that state of belief.

A lot of people believe that they are poor. I used to believe that, too. The proofs were there, practically incontrovertible. But it is not according to your circumstances that it should be to you, it is according to your faith. What do you believe? If you believe you are poor, you are poor. The force that comes from your spirit will control the material world around you to create poverty. If you believe you are prosperous, that thought controls your material circumstances.

Jesus was walking to the house of Jairus and was distracted by the woman with the issue of blood. You know the one—she took her miracle without permission. That is permitted in the economy of faith. Then while Jesus was listening to her testimony, somebody came from Jairus' house and said to Jairus, "Do not bother the Master anymore, the girl is dead." And that is the challenge with us human beings. We respond to the environment; we respond to the things happening around us. We define ourselves by our material reality; we accept as the ultimate truth the circumstances of our lives. We need, rather, to rely on our spiritual selves.

Once this man was told that the girl was dead, his faith flew out of the window. He was going to become depressed; he was going to accept her death as the ultimate truth. But instantly Jesus stepped in. Jesus said to him, "Do not be afraid; only believe." This man had faith. He was the one who came to invite Jesus to his house. And then somebody brought bad news and his faith was about to disappear. God will not help someone who does not have faith. In other words, he will not help someone create a situation that is contrary to the situation that is in the person's heart. That is it. So Jesus quickly stepped in and said, "Do not be afraid."[3]

I say to you also, do not entertain fear. Do not entertain anxiety. Let me ask you: what are the emotions you feel in respect to money? Presently, given your financial situations or circumstances, the issues with your accommodation, your education, finances, career, whatever it is, what do you feel right now about money? Is it fear, is it anxiety, is it worry, is it doubt? I used to worry a lot about what was going to happen and what was not going to happen. Was I going to be able to afford to do something or not? Conquering negative thoughts and believing what God has said began the process of change for me. So what Jesus said to Jairus is what I say to you. Do not be afraid. Let us run those negative emotions out of our lives. Only believe. Accept what God is saying as your reality.

THE FIGHT OF FAITH

There is something called the fight of faith, and it is something that happens inside you. It is the conflict between the reality of your circumstances and the truth of what God is saying about your situation. It is up to you to take what God has said and to accept that as your reality or to accept what your situation is saying. There is a statement I make often, and have mentioned it already twice in this book, "I can never be poor again the rest of my life." These days it's easy for people to think that I say that because I am blessed materially. But if you listen to some messages that I preached thirteen or fourteen years ago, you will find that it is what I said then that I am still saying now. And the way I said it then is the way I am saying it now. It is the same conviction. It was my fight of faith.

I defied my circumstances and chose to believe what God has said about me. I said it before I saw it. I said it when saying it made me sound like I was crazy. I said it when it did not make sense to say it. I told people even when I was jobless that I would not be a local champion, and that they should watch out for me. I said I was going to the world, even though at that time traveling between two towns was not easy. I believed then and now that, "we walk by faith, not by sight."[4] What do you believe?

This issue of believing contrary to your circumstances is an exciting one. I learned it from my pastor years ago, because even when he was riding on a motorbike, he was bragging on faith that our church was not a mushroom church; it was a *much room* church. He said he was going to the world; and right before our eyes, what he said came to pass after some time.

Now, it is your turn, it is your choice. You can look at the circumstances in your country, look at your background, look at the capability of your parents, look at your educational qualification or the circumstances surrounding your life and define yourself by what has happened in your life until now—or you can choose to believe in spite of your circumstances. Once the belief in my heart began to change, the words of my mouth also began to change; and somehow, all the excuses that I had given began to dissolve. I just realized that there was no reason in the world why I was not going to prosper.

At a point, I began to apply a Nigerian proverb that says, "If you pound yam in leaves and prepare soup in groundnut shells, as little as they will be, the person who will be satisfied, will be satisfied." That implies that however poor they say a country is, some people will still prosper in it. So I adapted that proverb and said to myself, "If they pound Nigeria's yam in leaves and prepare its soup in groundnut shells, I will be satisfied." Well, it's been working for me. It will work for you, too, no matter your country, because principles have no respect for persons.

What do you believe? That you are poor or that you are rich? If Jesus said to you what He said to those blind men, "According to your faith let it be to you," what will happen to you?

MONEY MYTHS

The following are seven myths about money. Carefully consider the wisdom of putting these myths out of your mind once and for all.

1. I need money to make money. A lot of people believe that they need money to make money. This is a dangerous belief. By now you realize that real wealth extends well beyond cash. You do not need money to make money. Some people who make the largest amount of money are people who do not start with money. There are many millionaires around the world who started with nothing—but they had spiritual wealth; I mean ideas and faith. Some people do not believe that they deserve to be wealthy. They believe that other people do, but not them. In fact, if they ever prosper by chance, that would be the ninth wonder of the world.

Let me emphasize that God is no respecter of persons. He created you as valuable as everybody else on this planet. And if anybody deserves to be prosperous, you deserve to be prosperous—especially because Jesus secured the qualification on your behalf. So if Jesus deserves to be prosperous, you deserve to be prosperous. The right that Jesus has to walk into the Father's presence is the same right that you have. Where He sits is where you sit, according to the Scriptures.[5]

2. Money is the root of all evil. Money is bad or money is good: which do you believe? The truth is that money is neutral—but it does take on the character of the person who holds it. One person has a thousand dollars and gives it to an orphanage; another has a thousand dollars and buys cocaine. The same amount of money. One ends up doing good, the other ends up doing bad. The problem is not with the money. It is the character of the person that determines the character of the money.

3. Building wealth is difficult. Some people believe that it is difficult to make money. When you have experienced deprivation, and your credit rating is so bad you can't even find someone to loan you a hundred dollars, it's difficult not to believe that it is difficult to get money. You will be surprised when you begin to attract a lot of money that it does not take extra effort. In fact, the same effort that some people make to be poor is the exact effort some people make to be rich. It is just that most people do not realize that they are actually exerting their energy for poverty. The difference between the two is what they think. It is in what they believe deep down in their hearts.

4. All I need to be rich is just one lucky break. Many people believe in luck even if they do not admit it. They sidestep seemingly small opportunities of life, let the days pass by and hope for the big break. But anybody who understands how wealth creation works, knows it is just like going through different cycles of sowing seeds and harvesting, and you experience exponential increase along the way.

5. It is not acceptable for me to be wealthy when other people around me do not have enough. Some of us feel guilty for being prosperous when our friends do not have enough. In fact, that is why some people are unable to build wealth because they are unable to resist any demand whatsoever that comes from them. This is more prevalent in the developing parts of the world where there are no systems to guarantee the provision of basic needs for the average citizen.

6. Rich people are fraudulent. Some people watch wealthy people drive their fine cars and you can see in their eyes that they are not happy. In fact, some hiss because they believe that those rich people are thieves. Given their experiences, they do not believe that anyone can make that kind of money legitimately. Take note, once that is programmed into your heart, you are in trouble. As long as you have programmed in your mind and heart that you do not belong to that class of "thieves," your mind will not work creatively to create that level of blessing. Gratefully thank God you are not a thief and that you are prosperous.

7. Having a lot of money creates a lot of problems. Some people look at the lives of wealthy people and what they see are the imperfections in their lives, as if being wealthy means your life will be perfect. They point out what went wrong with their career or health as if the same trials do not happen in the lives of poor people, too.

What you believe controls how you behave, and how you behave ultimately controls what you become. Whether you are conscious of it or not, what you believe deeply on the inside will control your behavior. I like that man who Jesus told, "If you can believe, all things are possible to him who believes." The man said, "Lord, I believe." And then he said, "Help my unbelief."[6] Sometimes that has to be our prayer. "Lord, I am up against mindsets and strongholds that are limiting my capacity to dream. I am up against experiences that have stamped indelible marks with scars on my heart. I am up against fears and anxieties created by real experiences. You need to help me to defeat and go beyond them to believe that my future will be all right and that I am prosperous." I pray that God will help you cross that line from lack to abundance, if you haven't already.

RECOGNIZE THE RESOURCES AROUND YOU

Real wealth is more than physical cash, so we need to learn to recognize our resources. I want to challenge you from today to think beyond money—instead, think resources. When you think in terms of resources, you will see that you are not poor at all. The fact that you do not have cash is no proof that you do not have wealth. God has blessed every country. Some have arable land; that is land on which crops can be cultivated. There is no reason in the world why they should not feed themselves. If you want to make money, you have to be conscious that God has given us plants and animals. Some people cultivate animals and make money.

God has also given us mineral resources. In Nigeria, for example, it was discovered that every one of the thirty-six states that make up the nation has at least two types of minerals present. That is exciting; that is money; that is wealth. And, of course, there is crude oil for which the country has a reputation internationally. Other countries worldwide have gold, diamonds, or bauxite deposits.

Then you can consider physical assets that you have. You may have land, or a house. You may have electronics or furniture. They have value and can be converted to cash whenever you want. You may have cash in the bank. I want you to begin to think in terms of resources. You have something to start with. Note that what has been listed thus far are tangible resources.

Then you also have intangible resources. Words are resources. When you read the Bible you will see the power in words. If you have words, you cannot call yourself poor. "A man's belly shall be satisfied with the fruit of his mouth."[7] Can you see that? Your mouth can produce fruits. And in the beginning, God used words to create the whole world. So if you are poor in words, you are poor. That is why I said when people have prosperity consciousness, when they have wealth in their hearts, you will see it in their words. Words are resources. Poor people do not know that. Hang around wealthy people, and you will see that the way they talk is different from the way poor people talk. Poor people do not see words as part of their wealth.

Ideas are resources; they have value. Whenever you think about thoughts, always bear this in mind, that in the intangible world, thoughts are things. They have real value. That is why your creative ideas are labeled your intellectual property. When you think in terms of resources, you will never call yourself poor again. I may not have cash in the bank, but I have words and ideas.

Then there is time. You have twenty-four hours every day that you can convert to money, because time is a convertible resource. In reading this book right now, you are converting time into wisdom. Please become conscious of the resources at your disposal. You will not feel poor. Remember, being poor is only a state of mind. Least of all, you have your physical energy. You can wash a car, carry chairs, run, swim, or jump as an athlete. You can offer a service or solve a problem. And that can give you a starting point.

Esau had real wealth, the birthright; Jacob had one pot of stew. Because he was conscious of the value of his resources, Jacob used the little pot of stew that he had to take the wealth away from Esau. Once in your mind you believe you are poor, you make God a liar and you discount the resources He has placed at your disposal. Always remember that money is only a means of exchange, and you have something to bring to the table. I have seen people trade ideas for money.

Do you remember what Jesus said when He wanted to feed the crowd? He asked His disciples, "What do you have there?" They said, "There is a young boy here who has five loaves of bread and two fishes."[8] He said bring them—because intangible wealth always needs a point of contact in the material realm for conversion into the material.

Let me explain that. Were all the trees that we have in the world now in existence when Adam was living on earth? Of course they were not. I mean the real physical trees that are six thousand years old. If you eat corn today, did Adam eat from the same stalk? No. So the ones we have now, where did they come from? They came from seeds that were planted. And those seeds, where did they come from? They came from seeds that were planted before them, right? So if Adam held a corn seed in his hand, God had quintillion tons of corn seeds in the invisible realm, but they all needed a seed, a physical material seed to be planted for some of those in the invisible realm to come into the visible realm. They have all been created in the invisible realm, but they need something, a point of expression in the material.

So when you are smart, you do not despise your resources. This is because you can always use the little resources you have to create a channel for invisible wealth to find expression in the material world. That was what Jesus did with the five loaves of bread and the two fish. You just need a small point of contact somewhere. Do not despise your resources. You are wealthier than you think.

In my book, *Start with What You Have*, I share insights from the story of a widow whose husband had just died and creditors came to take her sons to become slaves. She ran to the prophet for help. The prophet said to her, "Woman, what do you want me to do for you?" Then he said, "What do you have in the house?" The woman said, "Your handmaid has nothing in the house." That is how all of us think; I have nothing. Then she said, "Except a small jar of oil."[9]

We all need something to start with, and God will not allow us to get to the point where there is nothing around us that He can use to move us to the next level of breakthrough. We have gifts, talents, skills, and knowledge. We have relationships. They are all resources. That woman said, "Nothing, except…" I want you to become conscious of that "except." That thing that you have been overlooking that you did not realize could have commercial value could be the key to your wealth. God will help you to find it.

Wealth Is Created

To create means to bring into existence something that has never existed before. Once you develop the capacity to invent or create things, you can never be poor again for the rest of your life. In other words, if you don't have what you want, you can use what you have to produce what you want.

The first introduction to God we have in the Bible is that He is the Creator. "In the beginning God created."[10] The fifth word in the Bible is the word created. Almighty God has the capacity to bring into existence things that have never existed before. Anyone who has such a capacity is wealthy. This is because that person will always be able to produce something that he or she can use to exchange at the market. And when God created man,

He said, "Let Us make man in Our image, after Our likeness: and let them have dominion."[11]

Wow! You and I are co-creators with God. We have the God-given capacity to invent things. You are more powerful than you think you are. I know our environment can influence our growth, and a seed needs the right environment to blossom. The big problem with those of us who grew up in the developing world, or underdeveloped world, or even those raised in the ghettos of developed countries, is that our environment conditions us to believe that we are powerless, helpless, and poor. We are not. It is a lie. We may have been deceived for so long, but now deception has come to an end. If you have all of those resources I have been listing—and you do—then you are not poor.

You are too loaded with blessings to fail. Change the way you see yourself. You are royalty. When you walk, walk with your shoulders square. When you walk down the street and they talk about the common person, you have left that class—people like you are not common.

One day I was saying to someone, "Don't mind those rich people." And the Holy Spirit spoke to my heart. "You said, 'those rich people,' so who are you? Classify yourself." I thought about it and said, "Lord, I'm sorry." I said, "Lord, I am rich." So I began to tell people, "If you hear anybody anywhere talking about 'those rich people,' they are talking about us." You see, just a little internal change can make a world of difference.

We are co-creators with God. There are so many things that God could have done during the initial creation in Genesis that He did not do. When He made trees, He could have made furniture, but He did not. When He created cotton in the fields, He could have made shirts for Adam, but He did not. When He put wool on the back of sheep, He could have put a coat on the back of Adam, but He did not. He embedded many of the things that Adam would need for comfort in nature and left them that way.

He could have created all the computers that we would ever need in this world, but He did not. He could have built all the buildings that we would need in our world, but He did not. He could have built all the jumbo jets, but He did not. Why? If He had done everything, you and I would have been jobless. We would have had the capacity to create things, but there would have been nothing to create. He did only the basic job and left the rest for us.

The most valuable asset on planet Earth is humankind. Even in the creation of man, God could have created ten billion human beings at the same time, and He could have breathed into their nostrils, and all ten billion would have stood on their feet. In fact, He could have made them of same height, weight, and age. No one would have a father, mother, uncle, brother, or aunty. But he did not. He created only the first man and the first woman and left the rest of the job to us. So we are co-creators with God even in the creation of human beings. We are more powerful than we think we are. God designed that Adam would have fellowship with Him, and He would transfer visions, dreams, and ideas into Adam's mind. Then Adam would look at those resources and see the possibility for inventions in them. As a result, for example, he would cut down the tree and bring his chair out of it. That was the idea.

God worked six days and rested on the seventh. But I do not think that was true for Adam. From the biblical account, Adam may have been created on the sixth day. In which case, his first full day was the day of rest. It was a day of interaction with God and whatever creative ideas he got from the interaction would give him work to do for the next six days.

It is interesting to note that the most productive economies in the world have a culture of vacation. Why was the Sabbath so important in the Old Testament? It was one of the first commandments. If you broke it, you were stoned to death. Some of us who do not go on vacation live in some of the poorest countries in the world. Activity is not accomplishment. Activity does not necessarily result in productivity. It is the value that is released through the activity that matters.

God said, "Be fruitful."[12] In other words, cultivate seeds; do something with the resources He has given you. And if from this small quantity of corn you produce a larger quantity, you will have something to sell. If you plant a corn seed and you produce four cobs, you have just created four cups of corn and you have something to exchange at the marketplace. The value of what you create determines the measure of your wealth. When you create products and services that meet needs in people's lives, you get money in exchange—it is as simple as that.

The Word of God must have come from the thoughts of God. The basic raw material for creating anything is thoughts. Just look around you carefully; there is nothing that has value that humankind has created that did not begin as an idea in somebody's mind.

How God Gives Financial Resources

They do not spend naira or dollars or euros or the yen in Heaven. When you ask God to give you five thousand dollars, you are given the money in the currency of Heaven. Consider this illustration. Imagine that you need a thousand euro, and you have a cousin in the United States who is doing well. So you call your cousin on the phone to ask for a gift or loan of a thousand euro. Do they use the euro in the United States? No. They use dollars. However, your cousin can transfer dollars, the equivalent of a thousand euro to you because the dollar is a convertible currency.

So when you ask God for money, you should always remember that God is not in the business of producing counterfeit money. He will not rain dollars, euro, yen, naira, or shillings on you. The currency of Heaven is revelation. When you ask for a thousand dollars, God sends you revelation, the equivalent of a thousand dollars. This is because revelation is a convertible currency. "And the Word became flesh and dwelt among us."[13] That is conversion.

So when you ask God for money, He gives you revelation in the form of an idea, a thought, or an instruction. For example, Peter went to Jesus and said, "Master, they are asking us to pay taxes." Jesus said, "Peter, run down to the river and catch fish. The first fish that you catch, you will find a gold coin in its mouth. Use it to pay taxes for yourself and for Me."[14] Jesus gave Peter just one instruction, and Peter got money when he acted.

Second, when you ask God for money, you can call what He gives you vision. Vision is simply the ability to see things not just the way they are, but the way they could be. Vision is the key to provision. When we break down the word provision, we have pro and vision. Pro means for, and its opposite is anti, which means against. So if it is provision, it means it is for or toward vision. The word provision is another word for resources. It means that you only attract material resources to the size of your vision. If you do not have the vision, you do not have the magnetic power to attract the provision. If you do not have spiritual or intangible value, you are not entitled to have the material equivalent. That may sound strange to some people, but satan understands this better than many Christians.

When people pray to God for money, many do not recognize the answers to their prayers because what they are looking for is material. What God gives is intangible. So they continue the prayer and God wonders what they are talking about. On the other hand, imagine you were the devil—you are not—and you have made up your mind that nobody will ever become a millionaire in a particular family. Then somebody in that family becomes a born-again Christian and now has the power of the Holy Spirit. He prays and God answers; God gives him a revelation that is worth a million dollars. If you were the devil, and you do not want the person to prosper, what would you do? Wait till the revelation has been converted to a million dollars cash, and then look for a way to blow the money away? No. It is easier to steal the revelation. If you steal the revelation, you have stolen the money.

Satan understands that when he steals our revelation or frustrates our obedience to the instruction God has given us, he has stolen our money. I pray that from today, you will not allow satan to abort any more of your God-given visions. That is why Jesus spoke to us in the parable of the sower. He talked about the man who threw his seeds around and some fell by the wayside. The birds of the air came and took those seeds away. When Jesus explained the parable, He said those birds are devils. When revelation comes, satan comes immediately and tries to take it.[15] This is because satan knows that revelation is invisible money; and when it is sown in the human heart, it births faith and ultimately attracts its material equivalent.

Are you in the mood to take back whatever the enemy may have stolen from you? With God there is restoration. Please *make it a priority to have fellowship with the Holy Spirit daily*, through prayer and meditation in the Word—this is the first step to regaining the resources God gave you.

When you pray, expect ideas, strategies, or instructions from God. Remember when Jesus gave Peter an instruction, "Launch out into the deep and let down your nets for a catch."[16] Peter did it, though reluctantly. And the man who had not been able to catch a fish all night was shocked to see fish swimming into his net. When Jesus gave him that instruction, He gave him the fish! Wow! When you consider it from that perspective, you are wealthier than you realize.

Several years ago, when our church was very young, I was praying one Saturday morning. We had bills to pay the following week, and I did not know how to raise the money. Given our normal income on Sundays, it was obvious we would not be able to pay the bills. I was praying, asking the Lord for a way out, when all of a sudden, He said to me, "If I give you twice your normal income tomorrow, will that cover your bills?" I said, "Yes, Lord." He said, "Why don't you ask Me to double your income?" I asked Him for double the income. On Sunday, our income was double the normal income. I thought the prayer was answered. At the Wednesday service of that week, our income was double the normal amount. I thought that was the end of it. But our income doubled permanently from then on. One word from God on Saturday morning changed our income. I am convinced that *intangible wealth is the foundation for tangible wealth.*

I remember a day in October 2002. I was at a friend's house in Houston, Texas. I had been trusting God for forty million naira (about $250,000) with which we could buy a facility for our church. After more detailed calculations, we realized that amount was not going to do it. So I increased it to one hundred million naira. While I was taking a bath, I asked the Lord, "Lord, how do we raise a hundred million naira?" Now note this: many of us miss supernatural provision because we have fixed our minds on how the money must come to us. That is a big mistake. One day I was asking God for the money with which to buy a car and the Holy Spirit spoke to me, "Do you want the money or the car, which one do you want?" I said, "The car of course." He said, "Ask Me for the car and allow Me to choose how I bring the car to you—either to give you the car directly or to give you the money to buy the car." Always remember that the person you are dealing with—God—does not spend cash, He spends resources.

So to continue my story. "How do we get a hundred million naira?" I asked the Lord. Then He spoke to my heart, "Don't build for yesterday; build for tomorrow." I said, "What is that?" He said, "Build a facility where governors can find it comfortable to attend services with their friends." I said, "Thank You, Jesus. Governors will be coming to our church." He said, "No. That is not what I am talking about. What is the vision that I gave you?" I said, "To raise role models." He said, "That is what I am talking about. It is not that the governors are coming from somewhere; I am going to promote the people in your church. I don't want to promote them to the point where the church becomes uncomfortable and they have to leave."

Instantly, I jacked up the figure and said, "Lord, give us five hundred million." Well, the rest, as they say, is history. It was an idea; it was a thought in the bathroom. But it became our reality five years ago.

You are one instruction, one idea, one supernaturally inspired thought away from your next level of provision. *Learn to ask God. Learn to spend time in meditation.*

Third, to get revelation, *listen to God's prophets.* If God's servants don't have a specific word for you, at least they stir up inspiration. I have been at seminars, conferences, and in church services where, while the message was being preached or the praise and worship was going on, an idea occurred to me, and I wrote it down. Or I received the answer to a prayer request.

This next one is important. We should have enough wisdom, as much as Jacob had, when he traded a small pot of stew to *purchase intangible resources.* When Jesus said, "Do not lay up for yourselves treasures on earth, where moth and rust destroy and where thieves break in and steal; but lay up for yourselves treasures in heaven."[17] He was simply saying that you can use your material wealth to procure intangible wealth.

A wealthy young ruler came to Jesus and asked, "How do I have eternal life?" Jesus said, "Sell everything you have and give to the poor. Then come follow Me, you will have eternal life." The man ran away. After he left, Jesus said that it is going to be difficult for people who are rich in material resources to enjoy the blessings of the Kingdom of God, because their esteem is tied to the material. Peter said, "Master, how about those of us who left everything and followed You?" And Jesus said, "Anyone who has left anything for My sake and the gospel's sake, in this world, would receive a hundredfold, and in the world to come eternal life."[18]

"Bring your tithes and offerings to your store house and test Me; see if I will not open the windows of heaven and pour you out a blessing."[19] That is the instruction that God gave Israel. And there are lots of people who do not do that. They think that pastors are trying to defraud them. Some have given some tithes and offerings, but they have not seen anything material coming their way. However, God calls what He pours out "the blessing." And He says that your physical storehouses and bank account cannot contain the value of the spiritual resources He is pouring into your life.

When you give your tithes and offerings, God gives you ideas, instructions, dreams, and spiritual power. I must add, though, that if you give your tithes and offerings, and you still believe that you are poor, you are frustrating the process through which intangible wealth can turn into tangible wealth in your life.

Let us explore the story of Jacob again. He ran away from home because his brother Esau threatened to kill him. He got to a place called Luz, and he had to stay the night there. He prayed.

> *Then Jacob made a vow, saying, "If God will be with me, and keep me in this way that I am going, and give me bread to eat and clothing to put on, so that I come back to my father's house in peace, then the LORD shall be my God. And this stone which I have set as a pillar shall be God's house, and of all that You give me I will surely give a tenth to You."*[20]

What was Jacob doing? He was making an exchange with God. The impact of this exchange on his material wealth was astounding. This is how he put it:

> *And it happened, at the time when the flocks conceived, that I lifted my eyes and saw in a dream, and behold, the rams*

which leaped upon the flocks were streaked, speckled, and gray-spotted. Then the Angel of God spoke to me in a dream, saying, "Jacob." And I said, "Here I am." And He said, "Lift your eyes now and see, all the rams which leap on the flocks are streaked, speckled, and gray-spotted; for I have seen all that Laban is doing to you. I am the God of Bethel, where you anointed the pillar and where you made a vow to Me. Now arise, get out of this land, and return to the land of your family."[21]

His boss, his father in-law, said to him, "Take care of my flocks for me. Your salary will be the ones that are spotted and speckled;" those were the lean ones, they were thin and skinny. So they would not mate with the fat ones. Laban separated them and took them far away. But when the fat, plain-colored ones conceived and delivered babies, they delivered spotted and speckled ones. So Jacob explained to his wives how their dad had changed the agreement on his wages ten times. When the man saw that the offspring of the fat ones were spotted, he changed the terms and said that the spotted ones were his and the plain-colored ones were Jacob's. Then spotted cows gave birth to plain-colored animals. Then he changed the terms back again.[22]

Do you remember what the vow was? It was that he would give God a tenth of his income. Jacob understood the law of exchange. He used the material to create a flow of spiritual resources. God blessed Jacob. People say, "I don't have money, that's why I am poor." It is not because they do not have money. Jacob traded with tithes he had not even earned yet. And because of that transaction, an angel appeared and punched some keys in the genetic codes of animals so they could produce what would make Jacob rich.

The employee became wealthier than the employer. Because Jacob's wealth was spiritual, he could not be impoverished. There was no new policy in the organization that could make him poor.

I declare that you are free from lack. Nobody—system, government, or boss—will be able to stop you from being prosperous. I declare that every thought, every form of consciousness and idea of your being in lack will perish from your heart and mind. God will use your meditation during the day and the dreams of the night to deposit wealth into you.

Chapter Four

The Real Value of Your Mind

Train Your Mind

What is the population of your city? I will use the population of London as an illustration. Please use the population figure for your city as we go along. The official population figure of London according to the Greater London Authority is about 7.5 million. How much does the average person spend on food in a day? Let us assume it is five pounds. When we multiply the two figures we get 37.5 million pounds. That implies that 37.5 million pounds is spent on food in London on an average day. Multiply that by thirty days and you have 1.125 billion pounds. If each person who lives in London puts on two pieces of clothes a day, it comes to fifteen million pieces of clothes worn every day. They use seven and a half million pairs of shoes and seven and a half million toothbrushes daily. Those toothbrushes need toothpaste.

Seven and a half million people need to use soap to wash in the morning, and they need soap to wash their clothes. They need houses to live in, those houses need electronics and furniture, the people need beds, the beds need mattresses, the mattresses need bed sheets, pillows and pillow cases, etc. A fraction of the seven and a half million people need to move around the city; that is opportunity for transportation every day. Some of the 7.5 million are children who need to go to school. Those kids need textbooks, notebooks, pencils, sharpeners, erasers, and rulers. Can you imagine the amount of money that is being exchanged daily in your city when people purchase these products and services? Which of the products or services needed in your city are you selling?

"There is a global economic meltdown," somebody says. "Things are hard. There is no money anywhere." Excuse me—money is flowing around you every day. The only problem, according to Robert Kiyosaki,[1] is that you do not see real money with your eyes, you see it with your mind. I pray for you to receive a new level of revelation, wisdom, understanding, and direction. You will know what to do to move to the next level of financial breakthrough. God will give you grace to recognize your opportunity. Where you failed before, you will succeed this time around. Where you have lacked, you will enjoy abundance. As old doors of opportunity are being closed, God will open new avenues for you.

Values and Money

As mentioned briefly before, a value is a principle or practice that you have adopted as a personal standard. With your values in mind, you measure things according to their level of importance. You prioritize. Your values drive your behavior. How you respond to a particular situation depends on what is important to you. Your values dictate your choices. Sometimes you have to make a choice between two very good options; either you spend time with your spouse, or you make more money. Both are very important. If you have to choose between the two, it is your values that will determine what your choice per time will be, because your values help you prioritize.

When you look closely at the word values, you see that it is derived from the word value. In the preceding chapters I have been sharing some insights about wealth creation. I have tried to prove that it is not the absence of money that makes a person poor, it is the absence of thought-money. Being rich is a mindset, and being poor is a mindset. With the abundance of tangible and intangible resources that God has provided for us, we are not poor; we only have people who believe they are poor. And Jesus said, "According to your faith be it unto you."[2]

The following are some intangibles that are values—and valuable.

Love as a Value

An example of a value is love. It is a principle. Jesus said it is the highest, first and great commandment.[3] When you adopt love as your personal standard, it becomes your value. So when you have to make a decision, there are two factors to consider, two proofs of love. The first one is giving, and the second one is forgiving. So if you had to make a choice between keeping something and giving it, you will opt for giving it, because love is one of your values. If someone offends you, knowing that you have a choice between forgiving him or her and holding malice, you will forgive. And this is because love is one of your values.

Honesty as a Value

Honesty is a very important value. We must say the truth at all times, and we must keep our promises. Today in our country, people sacrifice honesty in order to make money. Why are the Ten Commandments so powerful? It is because they represent powerful values. "Do not steal." "Do not kill." "Do not covet your neighbor's goods."[4] These values have served as the foundation for civilization for centuries.

If you have eyes that can recognize real money, you will see that the wealth of the average developed economy is founded on strong values. Honesty is a major value for developed countries. Their citizens are not perfect. They are human like everyone else, and subject to the same temptations. When a person is dishonest, the system punishes him or her. This is because dishonesty impacts directly on the economy. When people are honest, it makes transactions easier. There is trust. In the economic world, they say trust is social capital. You can transact business without cash if you are a person of integrity.

I visited a country where I was told that the level of trust is so high that even if you sign a wrong signature on your check, it's most likely you would be paid the money, because no one looks at signatures there, because of the level of trust. They do not expect the average person to forge a signature. Of course the system is also effective, and they'll get you if you break that trust.

When you break God's laws, you attract a curse. Some acquire money quite all right, but they have curses hanging over their heads. They have spiritual poverty. Don't steal. Rather, add value to somebody's life. Solve problems for people. That is the legitimate way to make money. It has been my observation that countries where there is dignity of labor coupled with social welfare programs and economic structures to support those at the lower levels of the society usually prosper. Countries where people who serve as cleaners or security guards are despised because of their status, breed desperation and corruption, and multiply poverty. The foundation of such nations is in their value systems. They value money and power over human beings.

Where the true value of humans is celebrated, all are treated with equal dignity. When a highly placed government official who steals is honored, spiritual poverty will multiply. A blue collar worker should clean with dignity and without any sense of shame, because whoever earns money legitimately has more spiritual value than a governor or president who steals.

Value for Work

Work gives us the opportunity to be creative and to release our potentials. It is the process through which we get things done and achieve our goals. Not all activity leads to productivity, but without action we may not be productive. Goals don't achieve themselves. Problems don't solve themselves. To create solutions and to meet needs, we must engage in productive mental and physical activity. Laziness and wealth creation are not compatible.

Value for Life

"You shall not murder."[5] God has clearly commanded that we should value human life. Human beings are more important than money. They are more important than power and structures. The factors central to the wealth of a nation are human beings, and they need to be treated with dignity—everyone including children. All human beings are equal in God's sight. When a nation values human life, it uses state power to protect people who are most vulnerable. These would usually include women and children, and those with physical disabilities. In my opinion, there is no amount that is too much to spend to protect a person's life.

No Values, No Value

Dr. David Oyedepo[6] said, "If you don't have values, you don't have value." Anyone who violates God's principles and values to acquire wealth is creating spiritual poverty. Some poor nations do not know that their inability to develop world class infrastructure like roads, schools, hospitals, or power supplies are the result of spiritual poverty. When you go to the parts of the world where things work, you realize it does not take rocket science to construct a road. It is not angels that build them. Human beings build them, and they do not bring construction materials from Heaven. They use sand, gravel, granite, cement reinforcement where needed, asphalt, bulldozers, graders, and compactors. The difference is in their values. Their standards, which are rigorously enforced, are higher.

There is no amount of money that will make a nation prosperous as long as most of its leaders and citizens are dishonest. The government may construct world class roads and building, such infrastructure will eventually be reduced to align with the quality of thinking of the people. Any leader who does not model and teach values will leave people poorer than when he met them. Rather than give vision and values, some leaders dole out cash to their followers.

Any leader who gives you values and models them is laying the foundation for your prosperity. Read the words Jesus said about money. He fought greed to a standstill. Apostle Paul hit at the heart of greed. He said, "Godliness with contentment is great gain. We brought nothing into this world, we will take nothing out. Do not give in to those things, for the love of money is the root of all kinds of evil which some people seeking after have pierced themselves through with all kinds of sorrow."[7]

A wealthy man ran after Jesus and said, "How do I inherit eternal life?" He said, "Keep all the commandments." The man said, "I have been keeping all the commandments since I was young." He was bragging. Jesus said, "I will show you where your problem is; sell everything you have and give to the poor." The man ran away; he was greedy. After he left, Jesus said, "You see, anyone who is willing to let go of anything for My sake and for the gospel's sake, in this world he will get a hundredfold, and in the world to come eternal life."[8] That young man missed it because his definition of wealth was wrong. He valued the material over the intangible.

Don't follow a leader who will not give and model to you correct values. If you come home from school with a pencil or ruler that is not yours and your parents discipline you, they love you; they are laying the foundation of your prosperity in the future.

If they overlook it because they say they love you, one day, you might end up in jail. You have a choice to refuse any influence that will corrupt your values. Some give poverty as an excuse for earning money the wrong way. However, Jesus said, "Do not worry about your life, what to eat, what to drink, what to put on."[9] Your life is more important than clothes or food. Do not compromise your integrity. Seek first the values and the principles that govern God's Kingdom and have right standing with God. Jesus said the food will come. Material provision will come to you because you have spiritual wealth.

There are some countries with welfare programs that ensure that people who are out of work get stipends from the government. Where that is not available, find a Bible-believing church to attend. If a church is built on the Bible, it will make sure its members do not go to bed hungry. It is told in the Acts of the Apostles, church members sold their lands and houses to make sure nobody went to bed hungry.[10] Once your basic needs are met, you can plan your life and start afresh. The people who are most vulnerable to crime in the society are those who do not have food to eat. Desperate people do desperate things. Be an active part of a church. And even if you get assistance for some time, make it your objective to support the church so it can take care of other people going through difficult times.

Adopt principles from the Word of God as your personal values. You will have spiritual wealth. Don't cheat. It will not get you anywhere. It can get you some money to spend now, but it has no future. It attracts a curse; and in a matter of time, that curse will take affect. There is no point in using cocaine or engaging in sexual immorality because you want to get a job. If you get the job, what you are giving in exchange is far more valuable.

Using Your Mind

Your number one asset for wealth creation, for converting intangible wealth to tangible wealth, is your mind.

In your composition as a human being, your mind is the bridge between your spirit and your body. The mind is the bridge between the spiritual and the physical. The mind is the conversion equipment. That is why Paul the apostle said not to let the physical world squeeze you into its mold. "Be transformed by the renewing of your mind, that you can prove what is...the will of God."[11] In other words, the spiritual provisions that God has made for you may never find expression in the physical unless there is an alignment in your conversion equipment. This is very important. That is why God will not do a thing until He reveals His secrets to the prophets.

When God wants to do something, He says it. The angel had to appear to Mary when Jesus, a spiritual reality, was going to be conveyed into this material world. The angel said to Mary, "You will conceive a Son." Mary said, "How is that going to happen when I have not slept with a man?" The angel said, "The Holy Spirit will come upon you, the power of the Most High will overshadow you, and the thing that will be conceived in you will be called the Son of God."[12] So the place where we fail is in conceptualization. I've heard it said, "Whatever the mind of man can conceive, it can achieve." The place where we really create wealth and convert spiritual substance into material substance is in the mind.

We have intangible resources like time, gifts, talents, and access to revelation. We have wealth. However, something goes wrong when we entertain self-doubt. Jesus said, "Whoever says to this mountain, 'Be removed and be cast into the sea,' and does not doubt in his heart...."[13] He was describing how we can make things happen in the material world. Many who have been favored with awesome opportunities have achieved little financially because of cowardice. Then you see people, who seem not to be gifted or advantaged, but who have guts, achieving great things. Sometimes when you act with courage, you surprise yourself. Sometimes, in fact, you exceed your dreams, just for daring. Remember God's initial words to Joshua, "Be strong and very courageous."[14]

Some have received many teachings and read many books about how to make money, but their circumstances have not changed because they have not been able to overcome fears and doubts in their hearts and minds. I pray that God will birth in you a new level of courage. When you can move mountains on your inside, you will move mountains in your finances.

How to Recognize Opportunities

Please remember, you do not see real money with your eyes, you see it with your mind. I am emphasizing the ability to recognize opportunities, and the equipment that you use to do that is your mind. How do you recognize opportunities? Oh, give them another spelling: P-R-O-B-L-E-M-S. Opportunities are problems that are around you in abundance. Some people are waiting for the big break, but when the big problems show up they run away. Problems and opportunities are the same. Find the connection between your skills and people's problems if you want to turn your spiritual wealth into cash. The place where you find that connection is in your mind.

As a pastor, I learned the hard way that the fact that there are millions of people in a city does not guarantee they will come to your church. We make a lot of assumptions in church work just like people do in business. We assume that if we can purchase a good facility, make sure the carpet is beautiful, and there is air conditioning, people will come rushing in.

Now what would happen if you saw a restaurant sign announcing that there are beautiful rugs, their plates are made of gold, and they have air conditioners—but no food? What would you do? All the beautiful furniture and decoration is of no consequence to you. The central factor of going to a restaurant is the food, because it cures your hunger. It is the same with church work. The microphone is important, but it is not the central factor. Jesus did not have a microphone when He preached to people, yet the crowds listened to Him.

There is something called people-blindness. It is the inability to recognize people's needs though we interact with them daily. We see people every day and something blinds our eyes from realizing that they have desperate needs in their lives. We need to develop the ability to recognize desperate and urgent needs. It is critical to our ability to recognize opportunities for making money. The tool for doing that is our minds, when they have been trained.

I love the biblical story of Philip and the Ethiopian eunuch. Philip was doing such an awesome job preaching in Samaria, and people were getting saved in large numbers. The Spirit of God said, "Move down to the desert, go to the road that goes down to Gaza." Phillip got there, and saw a car, sorry a limousine, actually it was a chariot, coming in the distance and conveying a powerful government official from Ethiopia—a finance minister today. As his chariot passed by, Philip heard him reading aloud from the Bible. In that instant, the Spirit said to Philip, "Join this chariot." So he ran alongside the chariot.

I like the way Phillip approached the eunuch. He explored the man's greatest need at that moment. Some people don't realize that rich people and those in power have needs. But they do. There is nobody in this world who does not have needs. Money is not everything, What defeats our thinking process sometimes is that we do not realize that not all needs are material. People have spiritual, emotional, and psychological needs as well as physical, material, and financial needs.

"Do you understand what you are reading?" was the question Philip posed to the senior Ethiopian government official. "How can I, unless someone guides me?" the man replied. Philip offered to explain it, and he was invited to come on board.[15]

Can you recognize people's needs? If Philip was into business, he would have sealed a deal right there. You must develop the ability to recognize people's needs if you want to make money. It is not enough for you to carry products around town; you must ask, do people need them? The more you develop sophistication in recognizing needs, the more money you are going to earn. Great opportunities are not seen with your eyes, they are seen with your mind. Let us discuss some tips for developing our minds to convert intangible wealth to cash.

GET EDUCATED

There are different kinds and levels of education. The important thing is to get education while understanding its purpose. Some people get education just so they can have certificates and get jobs. But the word education is said to be derived from the Latin word *educo* from which we have the English word educe which means to bring forth from within. The essence of education is the training of our inner faculties to recognize opportunities and to create solutions to problems. Some go to school and graduate, but they are not educated. The ultimate objective of education is learning how to problem solve.

When somebody has been trained for some years in medical school, what kind of problems will he or she recognize in society? He has acquired skills for solving health problems, so he can identify sicknesses and diseases. He has the vocabulary for articulating different kinds of pain. That means that those years he spent conditioning his mind in medical school have created in him the capacity to spot opportunities for healing. When a doctor solves problems, he asks for money in exchange for his expertise and knowledge—he is adding value to his patients' lives.

When you train as an accountant, engineer, librarian, biologist, chemist, or any other professional, you develop the capacity to solve problems. That way, problems become your opportunities to add value. That means that you have something to exchange for money in the marketplace. So please become educated. And don't just study to pass examinations, study to develop your mind. Develop the ability to recognize problems and to be able to create solutions for them.

Education can be formal, and it can be informal. You can serve as an apprentice. That way you learn through a hands-on approach, how to solve problems in a particular area. This kind of training is straight to the point. It is practical. Also, you can attend short-term courses to acquire or improve your skills. You can attend seminars. You can read books about your specialty. In fact, you must read to keep abreast of new developments in your field because knowledge is becoming obsolete at a very fast rate these days. Investing in your thinking ability is one of the greatest forms of investment you will ever make. Don't ask, "Is this course or book worth it?" Ask, "Am I worth this investment?" You deserve to realize your potentials to the highest limit.

Get Financial Education

After getting education, maybe as a teacher, architect, secretary, or whatever career you may have chosen, get financially educated. This is because sometimes you can recognize the opportunity to solve problems for people but not recognize opportunities to keep and multiply your money.

There are four basic skills you need to acquire in terms of financial education: accounting skills, investing skills, marketing, and some legal skills.

The first one is *accounting skills*; you need to be able to add figures. You need to learn some basic accounting vocabulary. You need to know what an asset is and what a liability is. You need to know what net worth means. Your expertise in any field is defined by your acquisition of its vocabulary. What makes a lawyer a lawyer is the vocabulary. *Sine qua non, locus standi, lacuna*—do you recognize these Latin words? If you don't, you will have to pay those who do. In the same vein, you need to acquire the vocabulary of the rich. It is very important. An asset is not just anything you buy; that is what people with minimum financial literacy believe. There are things you buy that continually take money away from your pocket. Rich people do not call them assets, they are liabilities. Anything that puts money in your pocket is an asset. Anything that takes money out of your pocket is a liability.

For example, your car is not an asset unless it is bringing money into your account. Otherwise, it is a liability. To calculate your net worth, add the value of all the money you have and things you own; subtract what you owe from what you own; and then you have your net worth.

There is also something called cash flow that you need to understand. It is managing your spending in such a way that you don't run out of cash. To create increase, we must have order. With basic accounting skills, you can have order in your finances. One of the most effective tools for creating order is a budget. A budget is a plan through which you can estimate your expected income and projected expenses over a specific period of time. You use it to control your spending.

Then you need to *develop investing skills*. This is the ability to get your money to generate more money for you. In the Parable of the Talents, the man who got one talent accused his boss of wanting to reap without sowing.[16] He didn't know that rich people don't only work for money; they make their money work for them. They invest in stocks, real estate, fixed deposits in banks, gold, businesses, and other investment vehicles. To succeed as an investor, you need to be able to assess the level of risk involved in each transaction, and you need to understand your own capacity for risk. Also, you need to understand how compound interest works and how you can leverage it long-term to multiply your wealth.

You also need *marketing skills*. You need to know how to sell something. I mentioned earlier that you need to find the connection between your gift and skill, and what people need. However powerful your product or service may be, you are likely to have difficulty selling it if those who need it are not aware it exists. I learned as a preacher that you can have the most powerful message in this world, and the most powerful anointing, but if you cannot direct it at specific needs in people's lives, they are unable to see how what you are offering will add any value to their lives. That is what marketing is all about—your ability to recognize people's needs and to help people perceive how what you have will meet those needs. That requires skills—marketing and selling skills.

In Robert Kiyosaki's book *Rich Dad, Poor Dad,*[17] he writes about how he was having an interview with a journalist in Singapore. She was a well-known journalist, and he had read a few of her articles; they were powerful, strong, and direct. But she was lamenting to him that people were not buying her books. Kiyosaki said to her, "I think you need to go to school; you need to attend a course on selling." She said, "That is one thing I do not like. Selling is beneath my dignity because I feel that what they teach sales people is manipulation. They just look for ways to manipulate people to buy things and I'm not interested in all that." Robert Kiyosaki said he observed that she was angry; in fact, she began to pack her papers, and that was the end of the interview. He then picked up his book and pointed to something on the cover as she was packing her bag. "That is it," he said. She said, "What? Best-selling author?" He said, "Yes. You see, I am a best-selling author—not best-writing author." So you can be a best-writing author and not be a best-selling author, and you will read your book yourself."

Robert Kiyosaki titled his first book, *If You Want to Be Rich and Happy, Don't Go to School.* When he gave the manuscript to the publisher, the publisher said no and suggested another title; the economics of education or something like that. Kiyosaki told the publisher, "Sir, if I use the title you are proposing, I will sell only two books—one to my family and the other one to myself." Kiyosaki did not take the publisher's advice and was deliberate. He said he was a champion for education, but the issue was that he wanted people to buy the book. He used his original title, and the book sold and sold and sold. People bought the book because the title aroused their curiosity.

If you want to sell a very bitter medicine, what do you do? You tell people, "Ah! Bitter, bitter, this thing is bitter." Even if you tell them it will cure them, the idea of bitterness will drive them away. So you coat it with something sweet. When it gets inside, it will do the job that it is supposed to do. Some people do not like us using marketing terminologies, like branding or marketing, especially when discussing Scriptures. I respect their opinion. However, I think it is just common sense to communicate with someone in the language that the person understands, while retaining the original idea. How come we hear God speak to us in our own languages, when it is doubtful that English, Spanish, French, Portuguese, Italian or any of our earthly languages has been adopted as lingua franca in Heaven? We should learn and apply marketing and selling principles, therefore, because we are dealing with human beings not trees and stones. And human beings, have emotions. We should, however, not abuse or manipulate people out of wrong motives.

Then you have to acquire *legal skills*. In every location where you are, there are legal parameters. You need to know what is legal and what is not, because you can make a lot of money but end up in jail. You do not want to break the law. There are always legal means of making money. And it is good to get the advice of legal experts because laws change frequently.

HAVE A FINANCIAL MENTOR

You need to have a financial mentor. I cannot tell you how much loss I have been saved from by having mentors. What will a mentor give you? He or she will give you ideas, information, and direction. In light of our discussion, what you get from a mentor is intangible wealth, isn't it? Come to think of it, it is stupid ideas that make us poor. The wrong kinds of thoughts make us poor. Really, when our definition of wealth includes intangible wealth, nobody is poor. Anybody who thinks he is poor is the one who is poor. The problem is our thinking. So you need to hang around people in the first place who will introduce some amounts of money into your mind that you would not have thought about on a normal day. Of course, it can be stressful and very threatening to hang around people who talk about millions like they are describing chicken change.

I cannot forget the day several years ago, when I was caught in a discussion between two ministers of the gospel who are in business and are also investors. They are much older than me, and they were discussing their investments. This was many years ago when my salary as a pastor was the equivalent of less than a hundred dollars a month. As they were talking, one of them described how he got a loan worth about $500 from a bank in the 1970s and bought a piece of land on which he later built a commercial property. He sold the property about twenty-two years later for the equivalent of about $110,000.

The other gentleman shared his own testimony about a building he had just sold. He said it had a penthouse and he sold it for about $300,000. The first man then mentioned a building that he bought some years back from the proceeds of the previous sale, and how some years later he sold it for about $200,000. He had invested part of the money again in a block of six residential flats, and it was now valued at about $300,000. I thought to myself, *I came to the wrong place today*. I was just smiling and nodding my head. They were stressing me out. They were stretching my mind. I was hoping they would not ask me any questions, because as far as their subject of discussion was concerned, it was completely beyond my range. That was not my area of influence, but I am glad that I listened because it was an encounter with the mindset of the rich.

There are stupid mistakes I could have made that I have not made, because I have developed some strong values over time, largely due to mentoring. There are things I would not do anymore. In reality, many of the things poor people do that they think will help them become rich are the very things that make them poor. Ignorance can be costly. You never rise beyond the level of your knowledge. So that is why I mentioned earlier that I have heard people say that a lot of money has passed from my mentors to me. In a sense they are right. But it is not the kind of money they think. It is intangible wealth. It is the counsel, the advice, the thoughts, and sometimes the inspiration that moves me to the next level of effectiveness.

The fact that I have the opportunity of going into an environment that is way ahead of mine helps to change my thinking, especially when I have the opportunity of going there consistently. At first, some of the things I saw blew my mind. But after going there several times, they did not startle my mind anymore; they became normal. I was thinking about this process one day and the Holy Spirit said to me, "When it has become normal in your mind, it has become normal in your life."

For we believers, we understand also that grace is transferable. Grace, simply put, is God's benevolence. You can get it from someone who has it, and its effects will work for you the exact way it is working for the one from whom you got it. For example, it was transferred from Jesus to His disciples and they produced the same results.

Several years ago, I was driving behind a Lincoln Navigator that belonged to a neighbor who was using it to take children to and from school. One day, as I was driving behind the SUV on the way home, I had the opportunity to meditate. Meditation is powerful. That is where your inner eyes open, and you gain insight. You do permutations and combinations either in your favor or against you. As I was looking at the car, I remembered that my mentor had one. I spoke out and said, "You, this car, I have the capacity to own you because my mentor owns one of you; and the grace that I am taking from him is not the one he had ten years ago, it is the one he has now. Because he has you, I have the capacity to get you. You will manifest for me in due season."

It was mentoring that gave me the opportunity to do such appropriations to myself. It is easier for me to see myself achieving what my mentor has achieved, especially because I can ask how he got his own. I want to encourage you again—please have a financial mentor.

Work Is Good for You

Work hard. When your mind spots a problem, it can design a solution. With your physical body you also have to take practical steps. Some people's needs are material, others are intangible. A car is a material thing; so is a microphone. A television set is a material thing and needs to be crafted physically. Food is material; it needs to be cooked, carried, and served. Some part of our work is mental, the other part is physical. Whichever is required, you must be willing to do it. Work is not a curse, it is a blessing.

God put Adam in the Garden to till it and care for it. He gave man work to do before the Fall of man happened. It was the productivity and the soil that God cursed. Work is not a curse. God wants us to work; He designed human beings to work. When we don't work, we function below our potential.

Work develops you. Work builds your character. There are qualities that work develops in you. You will develop the ability to set goals, the ability to drive yourself and to stay on a job. You are not perfect. Sometimes while you are trying to produce something, things will go wrong. But if you are committed to work, you will develop the ability to correct yourself when you make a mistake. Your ability to start again and to stay with something from start to finish builds perseverance in you. All the circumstances you meet in the process of achieving a goal change you.

When we talk about achieving goals, the reason why the life of a person who sets and achieves goals is radically different from the life of a person who does not have a goal is that in the bid to achieve your goal, you change. For example, if my income today is $1,000 per month, and my target is $20,000 per month, I have to become a particular kind of person to attract $20,000 per month. My capacity presently is attracting one thousand.

Every human being is a living magnet. So something has to happen to my magnet for me to be able to attract twenty thousand. In the process of achieving your goal, you stretch. A wise man once said that while the brick layer is building the building, the building is building the brick layer. When I teach people how to turn vision into reality, I say that the first step is to become the person in the vision. This is because the person is the magnet who attracts everything else in the picture. So working toward the achievement of your goals builds your character.

The lazy person who avoids work misses out on many things. All honest work is honorable. As mentioned previously, I have more respect for the janitor who earns an income legitimately than for an executive who steals. In the eyes of God, a person who earns a small amount of money is more valuable than a wealthy thief. It is important for us to know that. One of the reasons we miss opportunities to make a lot of money is because we despise what we call lowly jobs.

In my country there are people who offer basic services like artisans who fare better than university graduates. Once you go through our university system, it seems that something enters the graduates' brains telling them that offering basic products and services is beneath their dignity. And I think that the graduate who offers some of those basic services will rise to a higher level.

Money is no longer a mystery. It is a means of exchange of value. If you are willing to work and meet people's needs, money will come to you. And let me add this thought: do not work for money. Does that not sound strange? Rich people do not work for money. It is poor people and the middle class who work for money—and when they want more money, they work harder and longer. Do not kill yourself in a bid to make more money. Solomon said, "Labor not to be rich."[18] Do not increase the stress. There is no point in making more money and losing your family or your health in the process. Do not work for money, work to learn. Work for yourself. Work to achieve your goals, work to become the kind of person who will attract the kind of wealth you want. And you know that the key is your mind. Work to develop your thinking.

Some of the greatest investments that you will make in your life are the investments that you make into your thinking. That is where you will find the ability to recognize opportunities. So work to increase your expertise. Do not work only for a paycheck. Work to increase your value.

Do not work for a salary. It is something that I say to our staff all the time. A salary is one of the least rewards you will get for working. The greatest reward that you get for working is the person you become in the process of working. Some people work in an organization, and because their job title is that of an accountant or secretary, they get boxed in to that small corner of the job. And interestingly sometimes, they work directly with the CEO. If you have a vision to become a CEO, while you are an accountant or an administrator, don't just work for a paycheck—no. If your vision is to become a CEO, watch the CEO carefully. If you have the opportunity, read what the CEO reads, attend the meetings he or she attends. What are you learning? What makes the CEO the CEO is the way he or she thinks.

Once you start thinking at that level, it will show in the proposals and the ideas that you bring to the table in the organization. Some people have been promoted in organizations just because of the quality of ideas that they presented. In fact, for some people, they create a new department or a new subsidiary all together to test their ideas. Do not work to earn, work to learn. What you learn determines what you earn. Do not work for money. Rich people do not work for money; they make their money work for them.

As Robert Kiyosaki says, you earn money on four levels. You earn money as an employee, which is the lowest level. That is why I am encouraging you, do not stay there. You can also earn money as a self-employed person. That is when you start your own business and you are the only employee. You are the CEO, the purchasing officer, the marketing officer, the administrative officer, information technology manager, the accountant, the secretary, and the personal assistant to the CEO.

From there you move on to become a business owner. A business owner is someone who employs other people to do the job. You have the ability to build systems, design organizational charts, recruit people, train them, and get them to do the job. It is a completely different level from being self-employed.

And then the fourth level is an investor. You earn money as an investor. As an investor, you put money in places where other people are doing the job; they do all the work, they make the money, you collect your share.

What makes the difference between those four levels is the way the person thinks. Target where you want to be while you are still working as an employee or self-employed. Set your financial goals and personally decide where you want to be. If you want to make money, be wealthy and rich, then target the business owner and the investor levels. So while you are an employee, concentrate on more than your salary; learn everything you can about being a business owner and an investor.

The word that the Holy Spirit gave me that resulted in this book is the fact that He is raising up in our church, not just millionaires but multibillionaires, and in the name of Jesus the Son of God, I receive grace for you today. Receive capacity to recognize opportunities. Receive open eyes in the name of Jesus Christ. What others have not seen, you will see. What others have not heard, you will hear. The Spirit of the living God will inspire you in the mighty name of Jesus. The problems of your city or town have become your opportunities. Goliath was Israel's problem, but to David, he was an opportunity.[19] I prophesy in the name of Jesus that the problems of your nation have become your own opportunities.

Some people look at the population of Nigeria and they see 150 million problems. Some foreigners come in and see 150 million opportunities. I was in Canada sometime ago and was shocked when they told me their population. Canada is the country with the second largest land mass in the world. Yet its population is 31 million. But regardless of your location, you sell something to just one million people each year, and you make one dollar from each of them, that is $1 million. If you sell something to 10,000 people per day and you earn ten naira from each of them, if you do that twenty-five times every month—please do the calculation.

I believe that Heaven will deliver to you a solution. In your mind and heart, you will receive a design; the Holy Spirit will use your imagination as a receiving station for new inventions and creative solutions. Where people see problems, you will see opportunities. Where people's brains stop working, yours will receive creative solutions in the name of Jesus Christ. If what you need to know to be a problem solver is in a book, God will bring that book to you this year. Your gift will be exposed and your potentials will be realized. There will be a match between your gift and the needs in society when you value and use the mind God gave you. Just as people like Bezalel[20] in the Bible were gifted, so God continues to give people skills and talents to enhance His Kingdom and His children's lives. My God will give you the required skill for doing what is needed in your generation in the mighty name of Jesus Christ.

CHAPTER FIVE

The Spending Plan

Your ability to manage financial resources will determine the rate of your conversion of intangible wealth or the rate at which God makes resources available to you. If you are a waster with little, God knows you will be a waster with much. So it is a law—the provision of resources begins to reduce its rate when you do not manage your resources well. Remember what Jesus said in the Scriptures, "For to everyone who has, more will be given, and he will have abundance; but from him who does not have, even what he has will be taken away."[1]

HOW TO MANAGE YOUR RESOURCES

Planning

Planning is the key to winning. You must develop the ability to sit down and calculate the steps that will take you from where you are to where you want to be. You must make it a habit to hold a pen and paper while praying and dreaming. Think about it. When you have visions and dreams, the first expression that your vision has in the material world is on paper. When you write, you are pulling things from the invisible realm out to the visible realm. The place where the rubber meets the road, where your spiritual destinies first push out into the material world is in writing. If you pray for God to bless you and you do not have pen and paper in hand while praying, most of the blessings may slip through your fingers.

The prophet Habakkuk in the Bible prayed, "I will stand my watch and set myself on the rampart, and watch to see what He will say to me, and what I will answer when I am corrected." He continued, "Then the Lord answered me and said: 'Write the vision and make it plain on tablets, that he may run who reads it.'"[2] I translate that to mean, "Distill the intangible resources on the tablets." Unfortunately, for us in my part of the world, writing is our major area of weakness. Writing can be such a stressful activity for us—people in the developing countries. But Jesus said that anyone who wants to win in real life ought to win first on paper. "For which of you, intending to build a tower, does not sit down first and count the cost, whether he has enough to finish it."[3] We need to calculate and do the paperwork first, before we physically accomplish any goal.

There is a dimension of spiritual warfare that we have been taught. Most people are familiar with the aspect of dealing with spiritual entities and that is fine. It is valid. The existence of demons is a reality. However, there is another dimension that Jesus introduced. This dimension includes strategic thinking and planning, "Or what king, going to make war against another king, does not sit down first and consider whether he is able with ten thousand to meet him who comes against him with twenty thousand?"[4] If a king has ten thousand soldiers and is going to fight an army that has twenty thousand soldiers, should he run away? Not necessarily. Because it is not the size of the army that always determines victory in warfare. It is the superiority of strategy. If you do not win on paper, you are not likely to win on the battleground.

When you are fighting against the spirit of poverty, you must approach it on two dimensions. You must displace territorial spirits and other spiritual entities that may hinder the flow of your resources. Then also, you must have a strategy for acquiring wealth. You need to have a spending plan. In other words, write how much you expect to come in and how much will go out, and in what proportions.

Planning gives you control over the future. Things may not happen exactly the way you write them; however, you are better prepared to manage your circumstances than the person who does not have a plan. In fact, planning is one of the major habits or characteristics of successful people. People who fail, most of the time, do not have plans. It has been said by many wise ones that, "Most people fail not because they plan to fail, but because they fail to plan."

Planning prepares you for your opportunities. Everyone has opportunities. However, there are many who are not prepared for their opportunities. The person who has taken time to sit down, who has tried to envision all the possible scenarios both good and bad, and has prepared responses, will of course capitalize on opportunities faster than the person who has not taken time to think of possible options. Planning helps strategic thinking and maximizes your opportunities and resources.

Strategic thinking simply means getting the most advantage with the resources at your disposal. When you sit down to think and calculate, you can always win if you get insight and understand your enemy a little better.

Planning creates order and order creates increase. For example, if you throw your clothes into a drawer without folding them, the drawer will not hold as many clothes as when the clothes are neatly folded. So naturally, people who organize their lives and finances through recordkeeping experience better increase than people who do not. And planning also helps you develop the habits of the rich—like saving, investing, and giving. These are natural habits of prosperous people. When you sit down and plan your finances, then you can join the league of such people, like I did several years ago.

I remember when my salary was the equivalent of about three hundred dollars a month several years ago. At that time, I was invited to speak at seminars and conferences and would sometimes be given honorariums, the amount was unpredictable. There was a particular instance when I received a bombshell of a honorarium. It was two and a half times my salary for speaking at a conference! Oh my God! It was a breakthrough. Then a month later, Nike, my wife, asked me, "What happened to all the money?" Immediately, I became defensive. "I did not squander it. Everything I did with the money was reasonable," I said. She said, "I'm not accusing you of anything; I'm just asking what happened to the money." So I calmed down.

Sometimes when people become aggressive, it is a smoke screen. They are avoiding accountability. I said, "Okay, let me give you an idea of what happened to the money." Then I drew up a budget. Some people do their budget after they have spent the money. That was what I did in this instance. So I began to list what I did with the money. I was able to account for most of it, but certainly not all. Our brains are porous. Don't think you are that much of a genius when it comes to recalling every cent you spent in the past thirty days. Likewise, I could not remember everything, but I accounted for most of it.

When I looked at the whole list, I was a bit embarrassed because I had not spent an extra dime on our home. Instead, I had spent most of the money responding to urgent needs and requests presented by other people. And the money went just like that. Not that it was bad helping others, but there were other priority items I should have taken care of also. The problem is that I did not plan where the money should go before it came.

The Spending Plan

I know that some people believe, especially some cultures in parts of Nigeria, that there is a demon spirit that takes money from people as soon as they get it, and spends the money. If you have been spending money without a budget, try to recall your income and your expenses in the past thirty days. You will get a big revelation; you are that spirit. You are the one who has been spending everything. I hope you get the message. Don't blame any spirit when you are not doing what you should do. Planning is winning.

Record Your Income

Record your income and expenses for the next thirty days. That way you establish the pattern and volumes of your income and expenses. Then draft a spending plan and classify your spending under different categories. If you have not done this before, if it is not your habit, the first thing to do is to take it slowly; be very deliberate. The next several decades of your life depend on this. You are laying a new foundation.

Write down every income that you will receive in the next thirty days: salary, child support, etc. Then write everything that you spend money on in the next thirty days next to the amounts. Record everything. That means that you have to carry your record book with you. And at the end of thirty days, group everything together. The income should be classified under some headings like salary, gifts, dividends, royalties, and so on. Likewise, the expenses should be classified under headings that I will discuss shortly. When you realize your general spending pattern, then develop your spending plan for the future.

I am going to run through some headings under which you should do your recording. Yes, this is spiritual warfare. You must not lose the battle against poverty; heed this advice. If you do not know how to write, get someone to do it for you and tell the person what to write on your behalf. But you must do this. We are laying the foundation for a new level of living. The curse of poverty is broken forever.

Income Headings

Under income, you have *salary, dividends, royalties, commissions, honorariums, gifts*, and so on. Some people earn only one salary, some receive two, and some work three jobs. Some incomes are described as *investment income*. They include dividends from investment in the stock market; rent collected from real estate or intellectual property; yields from investment in businesses; and interest on fixed deposits in a bank. It is good to earn investment income.

Please make it a habit to record your income. You need to do it every day for one or two months, until it becomes a habit. Remember, being rich is a habit, and being poor is a habit. Many people earn a whole lot more money than their official salaries, but a lack of recordkeeping does not allow them to realize how wealthy they are. And if you are married, please let the person who is better with numbers keep the financial records—this is common sense and not a blow to anyone's ego.

Expense Headings

Tithes: Smart people will tithe. I know some people have issues with tithing, but there are theological issues that I won't go into here. And maybe sometimes, pastors overemphasize it. The truth is that God will not die if you do not tithe. But every wise farmer knows that he should keep part of his harvest for sowing to create another harvest. When you sow those seeds, crops that are still in the intangible realm have the opportunity of crossing over into the material realm. So when we give our tithes, it is an opportunity for God to pour out more resources, more intangible and consequently tangible wealth into our lives. It ensures that we enjoy continuous provision.

Taxes: We will never successfully build beautiful, prosperous communities without paying taxes. It is a scriptural thing to do. "For because of this you also pay taxes, for they are God's ministers attending continually to this very thing. Render therefore to all their due: taxes to whom taxes are due, customs to whom customs, fear to whom fear, honor to whom honor."[5] Jesus paid taxes and made His disciples pay taxes. Please budget for it.

Savings: Next we have savings. This is a really big issue. You have to save from money that is coming in, and the best thing to do is to fix how much you are going to save before the money even arrives. Please make it a priority. Note I am listing it closely after tithes and taxes. Some say it is actually what you pay yourself from your income. Most of the money will go to others, though you will get value in return for most of your spending. Make it a habit not to spend everything you earn. If you spend everything, especially on consumables, you may never become wealthy. "There is desirable treasure, and oil in the dwelling of the wise, but a foolish man squanders it."[6]

Rent or mortgage: Having a roof over your head is critical to your peace of mind. Make that a priority.

Home maintenance: Under this heading we have items that you might not have considered. They include property or council taxes, electricity, water, telephone, Internet, cable television, insurance, and other items. Please list as many items as possible under home maintenance.

Food: This explains itself. It's high priority. Watching for sales, using coupons, and pre-planning meals helps to control this necessary expense.

Transportation: If you have a car loan, you need to budget your monthly payment. I encourage you, though, to save to buy your car outright so you have no interest no pay. You must also budget for fuel, oil, and maintenance. When people plan to buy a car, sometimes they think only about the amount of money they will spend buying the car. They do not calculate how much they will spend every week putting fuel into the car. When multiplied over fifty-two weeks in a year, sometimes it can be a lot of money. You need to budget for that. Also provide for car insurance and periodic service checks. Sometimes you need to buy some car parts also.

School fees and/or child care: Under this category you provide for tuition fees for yourself or your children, and for child care. You will buy clothes, shoes, lunches, and other such items for the children. Lessons for music, dance, and sports also come in here, along with the uniforms, etc.

Entertainment or recreation: This is one area where that spirit works that allegedly blows away people's funds, which we spoke about earlier. Some people go to the movies. They pay for the tickets, popcorn, and drinks, but there is no record of such expenses, which can sometimes be quite significant. Some people buy snacks and soft drinks every day, and they lament that they are broke. If they add up those seemingly small amounts of money they spend, they will be surprised. Please budget for recreation, eating out, movies, and vacations. By the way, taking a vacation is important; one of the Ten Commandments says you must "Remember the Sabbath day."[7] Take a break once in a while. But if you don't want go broke because of rest, budget for it.

Pets: I mention this because it is one of those areas people overlook. Dog food, cat vitamins, and regular check ups should be provided for in the budget. In fact, how much did it cost you to buy the pet in the first place? I hope that was in the budget. Well, that is for those who love pets. The important point here is that you must budget every expense if you want to be in control of your finances. Don't give yourself sentimental excuses for being broke.

Debts: Some people owe ten thousand dollars and earn one thousand per month. But they will not pay anything toward their debt. They want to wait till the day they get ten thousand dollars before they pay off the debt. It hardly ever works like that. Do a budget. Whatever it is you can afford on a monthly basis, attack this debt and reduce it. I emphasize this issue of owing a little later.

Clothing: It's so easy to spend money here that we have not planned to spend. Window shopping leads to many temptations. The good thing is, if you provide some money in your budget for clothes, shoes, purses, and perhaps jewelry every month, your wardrobe won't go old all of a sudden.

Medical: I pray that you will not have to spend money buying drugs. But if you are on prescription drugs, budget for them. And of course we need to take multivitamins. Prevention is better than cure. In countries where you have health insurance, it is good to include the premium payments in the budget.

Miscellaneous: These items could include visits to the salon, laundry, and gifts for birthdays and weddings. Remember the story I shared earlier about how I received surplus income and it disappeared—most of it went as gifts. I had no budget for how much I could afford to give to people. Many people fail in this area, especially in the environment where I live. This is because there are too many people with urgent and basic needs given the absence of basic infrastructure. If you are not careful, you may begin to pretend to be God, attempting to solve everybody's problems. In the process, you are likely to create fresh problems for yourself. You may end up having nothing. If you do not take practical steps to increase your financial capacity, you cannot continue to help others. Because you need to increase your capacity to give, you need to budget for gifts. And whatever you give, please make sure it is recorded.

Reconcile Your Accounts

Please, make it a habit to keep financial records. At the end of every month, add up your total income and add up your total expenses. Total income less total expenses equals monthly surplus or deficit. Know your financial state of affairs, and take practical steps to work yourself out of financial failure if that is where you are. As you build your wealth, you may eventually need people to help keep these records. Then these management habits can carry over into the management of organizations. Remember, being rich is a habit, and being poor is a habit.

DEVELOPING WEALTH-BUILDING HABITS

Spend less than you earn. One of the wealthiest men who ever lived said, "When goods increase, they increase who eat them...."[8] In other words, when your income increases, you enjoy the thrill for a short time. But you begin to add on new expenses till the thrill of the increment disappears.

One of the most important wealth-building habits that prosperous people have is to spend less than they earn. The wise King Solomon, said, "...a foolish man squanders it."[9] I will never forget the first time I heard someone explain that Scripture at a seminar. It hit me like a rock. I know you may be going through some struggles in your mind right now. "What do you mean? What if the money is not enough?" you might be asking. Well, as long as you spend everything, or even more than you earn, the money will never be enough. *Spend less than you earn.*

Exercise the discipline to cut some expenses off when the money is not there. You need to be hard on yourself. Tell yourself the truth. And tell people around you the truth, too. When you don't have physical cash to buy something, you don't have it. Stop pretending, and stop trying to impress people. We have too many big-acting men and women around town. They have nothing, but pretend that they do. They are struggling to maintain the toys that others can fund comfortably.

The way we live in Africa, for example, everybody in the village is either your brother or sister or cousin, or your mother's uncle's nephew. In other words, we are all related. And since we are given to throwing parties at every little occasion, we get invited to many ceremonies. Unfortunately, many people throw parties they cannot afford to fund. A few times, people have asked me for personal loans to spend on burial ceremonies, all in the bid to measure up to societal expectations. But must you have ceremonies that you cannot afford? No. And if you don't, Heaven will not fall.

Rich people are courageous enough to make hard choices. One of my mentors said to me, "I have been hard on myself, but it has paid me." The fact that the money is there does not mean we should spend it. Anybody who hangs around me knows that. It is the way you manage little that determines how much increase God will bring in the future. *Discipline yourself.* Tell yourself the truth; you can't have everything. Have the courage to say no when the resources are not there. You cannot meet every need; God told me, when I was always broke, that I couldn't keep trying to meet every need around me. He said, "If you pretend as if your middle name is El-Shaddai, you will soon discover it is 'I shall die.'" That was when I stopped overreaching myself and my resources.

It's been said by many that, "People buy things they don't need, with money they don't have to impress people they don't like." And here's another quote that also makes good sense, "If your outgo exceeds your income, your upkeep will be your downfall."

The message is clear; spend less than you earn, and your spending plan will work for you in many blessed ways.

Chapter Six

Breaking Free From Poverty

I have been on a quest to understand the spiritual technology for converting dreams to reality. Those who have access to dreams, visions, and ideas cannot be called poor. This is because the intangible world created the tangible world. The apostles said, "Silver and gold I do not have, but what I do have I give you."[1] They were conscious of their spiritual wealth, which made them free from having a poverty mindset.

So my quest is to understand how to access wealth like that in the intangible realm, and to know how to convert it into tangible wealth. We have discussed the important role of work, and the fact that the major part of the work that you do to create wealth is spiritual and mental. Then you must add physical work to it. With work, you shape your circumstances to align with your dreams. Well, I have a few practical tips here to help you see your wealth become physical reality, so you can be free from material poverty.

Increase Your Income

As you take practical steps to break free from material poverty, look for ways to increase your income. The starting point is to decide on your financial goal. You must have a definite financial goal. It is not enough to say that you want to make more money. That is not a goal; it is vague. Goals are specific. How much are you earning now? How much would you like to earn, and when would you like to achieve that level of income? Nothing becomes dynamic until it becomes specific. Specificity is critical if you want to move from where you are. Define exactly where you are going. Give it a deadline; it may be six months or one year.

And then read *Success Is Who You Are*, one of my latest books, and see there how to set goals, and how to organize your inner resources to focus on a goal until it becomes your reality. You will see how to write goals on paper and stick them on the wall or cut pictures from newspapers and magazines and stick them on the wall in your room so you can see them every day. You will see also how to write a check in your name and stick it on the wall where you can see it daily. And you will see scriptural proofs of how God changed people's lives through those methods.

For example, Abraham wanted children, but he was confronted with his wife's barrenness. God told him to count the stars and said that as many as the stars were, so would his descendants be. Abraham needed to have a picture in his heart.[2] So you have got to be specific about how much you want to earn. It is not a big deal, really. Somebody is earning that kind of money already. All you need to do is simply obey the principles of goal setting.

For example, I describe the basic principles as the ABC of goals—*goals have to be achievable, believable, and concrete*. If the moment you write a goal and give it a deadline and you know that it is unrealistic, you have failed before starting. *A goal has to be believable*. In other words, it must not create huge doubts that defeat you. Don't be a vague dreamer or a wishful thinker. Then your *goals have to be concrete*, and that means they must be specific; it is not a figure that changes every day. So decide on a definite financial goal.

Now, on a practical note—get a job if you are not working. If you are not earning any income, the first thing to do is to get a job or create a job for yourself. You have to be earning something. I know when we talk about getting a job, especially in times like these with the global economic recession where people are losing jobs, someone will ask, "What are you talking about?" This is where the battle begins. You have to be willing to run against the culture if you want to rise. Do not take what is said in the news and accept it as your reality. "For we walk by faith, not by sight."[3]

Second, I am aware that when we talk about getting a job, some feel that they are at the mercy of the person who is offering employment. That is unfortunate. I want to say that you are not. You have to see yourself the way God sees you. You are a wealthy person who wants to add some of the value of your wealth to an organization. You are not a liability looking for somewhere to attach yourself. Those who conduct interviews can sense whether a prospective employee is going to be an asset or a liability. It shows in the way they talk, sit, and comport themselves. I received a piece of advice many years ago that I should incorporate myself. I began to see myself as the CEO of Sam Incorporated. When I get a job, it is a contract. The CEO of Sam Incorporated has been hired out to another organization at an agreed price per month for offering some specified services.

When you get a job this way, it is with dignity. You do not have to lose your self-esteem because you are getting a job. It is a contract. It is a privilege to work and do your best to serve God and others. Employees need to know that the way an employer has the right to choose an employee, is the way an employee has the right to choose an employer. Remember what we said about work, that it is not the paycheck at the end of the month that is your greatest reward for working. In fact, do not work for money. The greatest reward for working is the person you become in the process of doing a job, knowing that God appreciates and supports a hard worker. Having said all that—get a job. Overcome inertia and make sure you are earning an income. "For even when we were with you, we commanded you this: If anyone will not work, neither shall he eat."[4]

Add Value

The core transaction that takes place when you have a job is that you add value and solve problems. You give out value that qualifies you for a salary at the end of the month; money is only a means of exchange of value. Do you have any value to add? That is an important question. People look for jobs sometimes and their focus is on the pay. But how much value are you going to give in exchange? The people paying the fat salary you want to earn have quantified the amount of value they expect from the person occupying the position you want. That is why they fixed that fat salary.

So the main issue is not the money; the main issue is the value. If you want to increase your income, then increase the value that you are giving in exchange. If you cannot find a place where you can be paid for giving value, find a place all the same to give value for free. Serve as a volunteer. You know why? You trigger a principle that can never fail. "Seed time and harvest shall never cease."[5]

Some of us have forced value to come back to us. Once, when I could not get a job, I went to offer my services for free. The place I found was the church, but it can be anywhere, a library, school, hospital, manufacturing business, anywhere. There are unlimited opportunities to give out value. The one disservice you can do to yourself is to say that because you are unemployed, you will sit down and do nothing. You should be wiser than that. Offer your services even if it is for free. Go somewhere and invest because *investment is the key to achievement*. Output answers to input. You can create wealth if you become an asset somewhere.

One of the young men in church did something interesting some years ago. He came to our house one day and said he wanted to do our laundry. I declined because our laundry was taken care of. He insisted that it was God who told him to do it. We did not quite need his help, but since he said it was an instruction from God, we allowed him to do it. He did the washing and said he was coming two days later to do the ironing. He has not come back since. Not because he ran away, but because the day after he came to add value in our house, he received a letter inviting him for a job interview. He went for the interview the day he was supposed to do the ironing, and started work immediately at a bank. I still see him once in a while. It was a remarkable experience.

Principles work when we satisfy their conditions. You don't have to wait for an angel to appear to you in the night before you know what to do. Find somewhere to add value. That way you will create a cycle through which value will also come to you. Go and offer your services in church or in a business or a nonprofit organization. Don't wait for things to happen, make them happen. Be sensitive to the needs of people around you. Someone may need help with babysitting. Someone's car may need a wash. And for some, it may be that they only need a word of encouragement.

Joseph observed that two fellow prisoners were looking sad. It was when he probed them that he discovered it was all because of the dreams they had the previous night. He served them by interpreting their dreams. He didn't seem to get any pay that day, but two years later, value came back to him. One of his former co-prisoners whom he had helped mentioned his name in the palace and within a short time Joseph had become the second most powerful man in the country where he had been a slave and a prisoner.[6] I see a turnaround coming for you, also.

DEVELOP EXPERTISE

When you have a job, develop expertise; because in every profession, people earn money at different levels. Shoot for the highest level, and do not focus on the money or the perks that people on the highest level get. Focus on the kind of value they are adding and the kind of problems they are solving. Then develop competence to solve problems at that level.

When I realized that my life assignment is teaching, I told myself that I have to develop my gifts and skills to the point where, if without notice, I find myself in the presence of some of the most powerful people in the world and I have only five minutes to talk, I would have something to say. That is the goal I set for myself—to prepare for opportunities. "Do you see a man who excels in his work? He will stand before kings; he will not stand before unknown men."[7]

The difference between kings and the unknown men is the level of excellence they demand and their capacity to pay. There are cooks and there are cooks. There are chauffeurs and there are chauffeurs. There are fashion designers and there are fashion designers. There are secretaries and there are secretaries. There are accountants and there are accountants. There are lawyers and there are lawyers. That may sound monotonous, but I am talking about people functioning at different levels of excellence and expertise. I see many people in the younger generation failing on this point. When you discuss business with them, the first thing they want to talk about is the money. They focus on what to get, not what to give. And many of them miss their opportunities.

I attended an event the other day and the organizer of the event said to me that he wanted to contract someone he was meeting for the first time to do the video recording. Someone had recommended him, but the first thing he wanted to settle was how much he was going to get paid. He mentioned a large figure. The organizer asked him to leave, he got out his own camera, replaced the battery, bought a cassette, and gave it to someone else to record the event. End of story. The first guy missed everything; he missed it because he was blind and his definition of money was limited to cash. His focus should have been on giving value. If you come across someone who is requesting your services and the person wants to bring up the money issue first, tell the person that you would rather discuss the money issue last (unless the person is not trustworthy). Let service come first.

How can someone appreciate how much you deserve, when you have not defined the value you are going to add? Ask questions, get your client talking, and then come with all the various creative and innovative ideas by which you can add value to the person. When it comes to the issue of money, you will have a strong basis for negotiating when people see the value you have the capacity to add.

If you need to take a course, please do. Read books and learn. When you read the book, *The Outliers* by Malcolm Gladwell, you will find a principle called "the ten thousand hours principle."[8] It has been discovered that everyone who has become outstanding in their field has at least done ten thousand hours on that job. When you begin to add all the hours that you have put into your line of work, you will find that the more the better. Like it is said, practice makes perfect.

PROVIDE EXCELLENCE

Do your job with excellence. I cannot stand it when a Christian does a shoddy job because I do not then understand the essence of the investment of the Holy Spirit in the person's life. How can you and the Spirit of God inside you do a job that your customers will complain about? Pharaoh acknowledged in the Bible that it was the Spirit of God who gave Joseph the capacity to excel. "And Pharaoh said to his servants, 'Can we find such a one as this, a man in whom is the Spirit of God?'"[9] Know that the people who buy your products and services are not stupid; they want value for their money. If you work in an organization, it is the same thing. Your boss wants value for your pay. Focus on the value that you are adding. Make sure it is exceptional.

God's Word has set a standard for us, and I think it is unbeatable. "*With goodwill doing service, as to the Lord, and not to men, knowing that whatever good anyone does, he will receive the same from the Lord, whether he is a slave or free.*"[10] Nobody will perform and not get a promotion. Be a sincere person. Do not cut corners. If you cut corners, it will catch up with you. Do your job enthusiastically and passionately. If this job bores you to death, leave it after you have another lined up. You cannot prosper doing what you are not passionate about.

The person who really guarantees your promotion in life is God. Everything you do, do it as if you are doing it for the Lord. Being a follower of Jesus does not cover up bad work. Spirituality is not an excuse for mediocrity. If you can speak in tongues while you are doing what you are doing, there should be God's extra blessing on it because that little extra is what makes you extraordinary. Do your work with excellence; do it better than anybody else. Treat people well. When you serve customers, treat them with respect and honor. Do not move around sluggishly and lazily. Treat people like they are kings and queens. Walk confidently, give value, and go the extra mile. Exceed people's expectations. Wow people, and put them in obligation to you. Let people wonder, how much did I pay that I am getting all this? That will keep them coming back.

More importantly, you will get referrals—referrals without expensive advertising. The most powerful form of advertising is word of mouth. And this comes from someone who has had a personal experience. People do not understand what happens when they treat people shoddily. They wonder why they lose their job, or why they are not prospering. It has been proven statistically that one unhappy customer will do you a whole lot more evil than the good that one happy customer will do. Bad news spreads faster.

FIND SOMETHING TO SELL

Add a new skill or start a new business. Employ yourself. Do not wake up in the morning and lie on the bed because you do not have a job and stay there till you have breakfast at noon. Put yourself in the mood. You are the chief executive officer of "You Incorporated." Get poised for action. Wake up when people who go to work wake up. Have your bath and dress up; and if you have nowhere to go, sit down at the table, get a sheet of paper, write and review your plans.

I am asking you to take practical steps to put pressure on your life. Put pressure on circumstances and break free from those limits that the devil has thrown around you. Remember one of Isaac Newton's laws of motion? All objects remain at a state of rest until a force is applied. When you move, things will move for you. Find something to sell; an opportunity to add value, however lowly you think the job is.

DEFINE YOUR FUTURE

I love the story of Jabez in the Bible. The whole of Chronicles is about family lines and family trees. Before his name was mentioned, there were chapters listing people's names, but the Holy Spirit made it in such a way that when it got to his story, there was a break. It was a break to explain why this man was a little different from everybody else. He was exceptional. And that will be your testimony, also. I do not know how it has been down your family line, but God will make you exceptional. There will be God's extra touch on your life that will take you beyond the limitations others have experienced.

The word Jabez means "in pain" or "he will cause pain." His mother named him Jabez, she said, "Because I bore him in pain."[11] She used the circumstances of his birth to define his future. Unfortunately, that is how many of us have been defined. The average person born in the slums or in underdeveloped parts of the world is defined by the poverty in the environment. And all are just statistics, just nomenclature; it doesn't have to be our reality.

"And Jabez called on the God of Israel saying, 'Oh, that You would bless me indeed.'[12] He was saying something like, "I am a descendant of Abraham. I am entitled to the blessing. The blessing that God spoke to Abraham about is mine. Why is my situation like this? I do not know why my grandfather accepted his situation. I do not know why my father accepted poverty as his reality, but I am not going to take this as my reality. Bless me indeed and enlarge my territory. These cultural limits that have been defined for me will not define my life."

I live in one of the most prosperous countries in the world—potentially. We are not poor. However, the statistics say 70 percent of Nigerians live below the poverty line. That is, they live on less than one dollar a day. Also, life expectancy is low. But my point is that it is up to you, no matter where you live, whether to see yourself as part of such statistics or not. Jabez chose to be different. I can hear him say, "You have been writing everybody's history, everybody looks the same—mine must be different. Devil, you did it up to now; it stops here and goes no farther; from here my lineage changes."

Dare to be different. Pray like Jabez, "Bless me indeed. Don't let failure define me. I don't want to be defined by current circumstances. I don't want to be defined by the state of the economy; I do not want to be defined by any recession. I want to be defined by my destiny; I want to fulfill my potentials in God." God granted to Jabez what he requested.[13] God will grant your requests, too.

SAVE FOR EMERGENCIES

As you begin to enlarge your financial territory, save for emergencies. Saving is a basic principle. Some of the most powerful principles that control our world are called the laws of the farm. What you sow is what you reap. The quality of what you sow determines the quality of what you reap. The quantity of your seed determines the quantity of your harvest. There is always a waiting period between the sowing season and the harvest season. But sometimes the world gets so sophisticated, we forget these basic principles, and we get punished for that. They are basic principles and are inviolable; they do not change. So taking something out of your last harvest to plant to create a future harvest for yourself is a basic principle. Any wise person who wants to have continual increase in finances must develop the habit of not spending everything.

When Pharaoh, the king of Egypt, had a dream, Joseph, who had the gift of interpretation of dreams, said, "Your dream shows that there will be seven years of plenty and seven years of famine. Now I will quickly tell you what to do. Do not eat everything," he said, "keep a fifth part, or twenty percent."[14] And we see the miracle that happened with the 20 percent that was saved over seven years. The value exploded during the years of famine. When people were desperate to buy, that was when Egypt was in the position to sell. That is life.

If you want to break free from the spirit of poverty, I will tell you part of how that spirit works. When that spirit is after you, it makes you want to spend everything that you are getting, and if possible, even more. It makes you want to eat all of your harvest including what you should sow for your future. Do not spend everything.

Experts say we should save at least 10 percent of our income. Joseph saved 20 percent. That is aggressive saving. Even if you have to start with 5 percent, make it a priority to save something.

Let God's principles work for you. I know that sometimes the money is not enough to pay our bills. That was my experience. I understand what it is like for the money you have not to cover your bills. The big question now is how the money will ever cover the bills if you do not break out of the cycle. And you have to leverage on the power in principles to tame this lack that is trying to keep you in poverty. It is a principle. Do not spend everything, save some, even if it is 1 percent. Keep something back.

Tell poverty, "All the reasons and excuses you are giving me for spending everything are excuses for poverty, and I am done with you." Take some of the money out, look at it, and prophesy over it. And tell the devil, "Shame on you, I will not spend it. I am free." That is where the battle is if you want to break free from the spirit of poverty. You have got to keep some; do not spend everything.

Once you have a job, estimate your monthly expenses and save up two to six months' equivalent. If you can save up for one month's expenses, that is your first major milestone. Congratulate yourself. Keep it somewhere safe. You will be surprised how the spirit of poverty will look at you and be powerless to hurt you. It is difficult to feel broke when you have some money "breathing" in the bank account. If you can put the equivalent of six months' living expenses in there, fantastic! This will serve as emergency funds to prepare you for unforeseen opportunities or expenses. There are situations and times that ruin people or put them in very desperate circumstances and they find themselves in an emergency situation with no backup plan. Most people who have jobs are just two to three weeks away from being flat broke though they earn good salaries. Reason: they have no savings.

My personal experience with savings started the day someone spoke at a seminar for just ten minutes on a verse from the Book of Proverbs. I referred to that verse earlier. It says, "There is desirable treasure, and oil in the dwelling of the wise, but a foolish man squanders it."[15] This minister said, "If you spend everything that is coming to you, you are a fool." I would have gotten angry but for the fact that it was the Bible he was teaching. He said, "I am not the one who said so; it is Solomon who said so in the Bible."

It was difficult for me to come to terms that I had been a fool in that area of my life. The immediate thought that came to my mind was to justify myself. *What if the money is not enough?* I asked in my mind. It was like the speaker heard what I was saying. He said, "I know some of you say that the reason you spend everything is because the money is not enough. Now let me tell you, the fact that you spend everything is only proof that your wisdom pipe is blocked." It was as if somebody took a pipe and hit me on the head with it. I will never forget that day. It was a morning session at a seminar. When I got back to the office, I asked somebody to go to the bank to get savings account forms for me.

It is not the hearer of the word who is blessed; it is the doer of it. I opened a savings account and began to save. At a time when my monthly salary was the equivalent of about $300, I saw how much of a waster I had been, because within one month, I had about $1,000 saved up in the account, and all my bills were paid comfortably. I observed that as my savings increased, my income shot up monthly, and I began to keep money apart in a certificate of deposit. Our church income also went up, because I applied the same principle to the church's finances.

I had to talk to God about this exciting new financial breakthrough. I said, "Lord, it looks like I stepped on something powerful somewhere. Something is working for me that I don't understand. What's going on?" And He explained it to me. He said, "Before, when you were broke, you were broke both spiritually and physically. When you ran out of money in your pocket, you could not keep the thoughts and emotions of poverty away. You felt poor and you thought poor; and as long as you thought and felt poor, you were a magnet for poverty. But now that you have money in your account, when you run out of money in your pocket and the thought and feeling of poverty wants to come to you, you remember the money in the account and those thoughts run away from you." And He said, "As long as that account figure is in your mind, you will continue to attract that same value to yourself, because every human being is a living magnet."

Because this is spiritual warfare, you surely understand why the devil would not want you to save your money. He will fight you, throw all sorts of distractions at you, and try to stop you from saving. Put your trust in God to meet every need as you choose to do the Word. You cannot do the Word and fail.

Now as you save your money, let it earn interest. When you put money in a savings account, it earns interest. Do not leave it there; put it in a certificate of deposit. Taste what rich people taste. I did not realize how powerful this could be until I started it both personally and for the church. At first, monthly interest was some few hundred dollars for the church, but it began to run into thousands of dollars. I discovered that one can make money off a bank. I prefer this. As your money earns interest, let it be easily accessible. This is not the money you put in shares or stocks that may take you time to sell. This is liquid money that you can easily access when you need it.

LIMIT YOUR EXPOSURE TO ADVERTISEMENTS

Some people's motto is "This shopping catalog shall not depart from before my eyes; I will meditate on it day and night and seek to buy everything that is in it, for then I will walk my way into poverty." Hope you get the joke. That is an adaptation from Joshua 1:8 in the Bible. Don't watch too many television commercials or read too many advertisements. You may lead yourself into temptation. You bought the television set with your money. And you pay the electricity bills. So it should not become an opportunity for people to come and whet your appetite till you feel that your life is not complete without a new set of bedroom linens or lawn mower. Turn it off or change channels. You must be aware that marketers and advertisers are getting more and more sophisticated. A very high level of psychology and research goes into the packaging of products now. If you exercise patience, you will eventually get the things you need, without stress.

Develop Contentment

Don't be materialistic. Don't define your life by what you have. You are not what you drive. You are who God says you are. Yes, enjoy material things, but for God's sake, if they are not available, be contented all the same. In a poor environment, it is the easiest thing in the world for people to get hung up on material things. Then when those things are no longer available, people become desperate. This is because they have been used to giving people the impression that they are big men. They continue to drive a car around that they are borrowing money to fuel. Of what use is that? They are not the ones driving those cars, those cars are driving them. There is no point suffering while smiling to impress people. From the first day you buy a car, its value begins to go down. In the language of the rich, that is not an asset; it is a liability, or a depreciating asset.

I know people often quote the Scripture that says, "I can do all things through Christ who strengthens me."[16] But read the whole context and the preceding verses. Paul the apostle said, "Not that I speak in regard to need, for I have learned in whatever state I am, to be content."[17] Give yourself time. Don't be in too much of a hurry. Develop contentment.

Pay Your Debts

If you want to fight poverty, you must pay off your consumer debts. There are two dimensions to debt—borrowing to consume and borrowing to invest. These are two different levels, and the unfortunate thing I find is that there are too many people who borrow to consume. In other words, what they borrowed money to do is not something that will bring money to them. It is not investment. It is money that is spent and gone forever. They spent their future income upfront.

God's Word says that the poor are always ruled by the rich, so do not borrow and put yourself under slavery.[18] Things seem easy with lenders at the point at which you borrow, it is when you need to pay back and you cannot, that you go through emotions of anguish, fear, and anxiety that you did not factor in before. But then, the money is gone. These emotions make it even more difficult for you to get out of debt.

Remember the widow in the Old Testament whose husband died? The husband had been a minister, but when he died, the creditors came to take his two sons away. A woman who just lost her husband was about to lose her two sons, too.[19] Do not sell your future, be very careful. Do not make it a habit to borrow money. Develop sound financial management habits. If you are tempted to borrow for consumption, fight that idea through prayer. If you have already borrowed money like that, I am encouraging you to get out of debt. Fix an amount that you will pay back monthly.

I have suggested that you should have the equivalent of two to six months of your monthly expenses in savings. However, if you owe money, keep it at three months' equivalent of your monthly expenses. Begin to offset your debts from the money you have been saving. Start with the debt that has the highest interest because that is the one that puts you in trouble fastest. When you borrow, interest is not your friend. Only when you are the lender is interest your friend.

If you have a car loan, pay it off as fast as you can. If you can, it is better to wait and save up for an item. Then when you are done paying for the car loan, ride or drive that car for at least three extra years while depositing the regular monthly payments into a savings account. And then after three years, take the money you have saved plus the residual value of the vehicle and trade it in to buy another car. Do not try to impress anybody. Focus on functionality. Of what use is a car? You are not likely to sleep inside it. It is something to take you from one point to the other. There are many things you can use to boost your self-esteem, but please, not a depreciating asset.

If you are in debt, I encourage that you accelerate the rate of cancellation of debts. If you have an asset that you can sell, sell it. Add the money to pay off your debts. Get out of debt as fast as you can. This is wisdom that will serve you well over the years to come.

In the event that you are finding it hard to catch up with your payments, please communicate with your creditors. Don't run away from the people you owe. There are some people who come to church and sit at the back or who know where their creditor normally sits in church and they sit at the other end, and then bolt out before the benediction. They make it look like they have a very important appointment to keep. Please don't run away from the person you owe. Walk up to the person. Have a plan ready for making payments. Let them know how much you can afford monthly. A borrower prefers to get a small amount from you monthly than to get nothing. So discuss with your creditor. Lay out your plan. Let it be reasonable, start to pay immediately. Please walk in integrity.

SAVE FOR MAJOR PURCHASES

Save for major purchases and for investment. "There are four small creatures, wisest of the wise they are; ants frail as they are, get plenty of food in for the winter."[20] Preparation, saving, and gathering—that is the strength of the ant. King Solomon said they are small, tiny, and physically weak, but they leverage on their brains. They leverage on principles. You can leverage on the power of saving to climb out from the hole of poverty. I have done it; I have practiced it; and I have seen how powerful it is. It works.

For a start, review your life purpose and goals. Take a long look. Okay, you have paid your creditors; now you have capacity to save money in preparation for the future. What is your life purpose, and what are your major goals? If you have not set goals for the next five or ten years, you will spend all your money now not realizing it is just seed money. Your harvest is not here yet, so take the long view and be aggressive in saving. As your income increases, peg your expenses. I know it will be difficult to escape the messages that come to you, because when riches are increased, so are they who eat them.[21]

Cyril Northcote Parkinson[22] established a law that states expenses will always rise to meet income. As soon as your income increases, you will find that when you walk into a mall or supermarket, everything there begins to talk to you, "Buy me. Exercise your power and put poverty to shame." You see, most of that will come from things you could not afford before. But, of course, many want to impress people. We think, *How can my friends come to our house and see an old, small television set?* That is how it starts, and before we know it, the salary raise is no longer sufficient.

To build wealth, you must fight to limit your expenses. So, when you get a raise, keep your expenses where they have been. That way you can enjoy the surplus. Save aggressively for special purposes like buying a house or funding your children's education. University education will be more expensive fifteen years from now; start saving for it. Savings give you leverage. Save toward starting a business. For those of us in countries where there is no easy access to credit, saving gives us leverage for starting and running a business, and for taking a business to a higher level.

Save for investments. Also save for retirement. Let your aspiration be for you to build your wealth to the point where the returns from your investments are enough to pay your bills. At that point, you don't have to work for money anymore. You work to add value. Do not plan to stop working. There is nowhere in the Bible people are told to retire, except for priests in the Old Testament who stopped doing the work of priests at the age of fifty.[23] Once you stop adding value, you may be on your way out of this world.

But my emphasis is for you not to have to work the whole of your life to be able to eat. If you have enough in investments, somewhere along the line, your returns from investments will be enough to take care of you. Keep the basic principles and be consistent. Do not save this month and skip the next three months. Be consistent. Take advantage of compound interest; invest your money wisely. And when saving especially for a business, be patient; make sure you have saved enough to tide you over the first few years. This is very important.

Please remember this—nobody owns anything in this world. God owns everything. He entrusts His resources to people. What you are doing with the little that you have today already indicates what you will do with more. Saving gives you leverage, it is one battle that you must win. Since we began to save in our church, I discovered that whenever we have some good amount of money in the account, it makes it easier for us to negotiate to buy things that are three or four times that amount. When the vendor sees what we have already, it increases the level of trust in our capacity. It gives us leverage.

Some years back, we bought a property worth about $3 million loan free. The negotiation was possible because we had over a million dollars in savings. Who would not want to do business with somebody who can afford to pay a deposit of over a million dollars cash? But you need to know what it takes to build up the funds. It takes discipline. It takes fighting your appetites. It takes you seeing the money and denying yourself some luxuries.

What I say all the time in our office is that money is not the solution to every problem. We need creative ideas. Jesus fed thousands of people with bread and fish. After everybody had gone, He said to His disciples, "Gather the fragments so nothing is wasted."[24] You see, once you waste the fragments, you will eventually waste the whole bread.

God has resources that He wants to entrust to you. Can you be trusted? Do you have enough discipline? Can you hold yourself? Can you see that you have the power to take something but refuse to take it because the Spirit of God has not given you permission to do so? The fact that somebody is your friend and he owes a lot of money is no reason for you to give the person money. Did God ask you to do so? That is the point. "As many as are led by the Spirit of God, they are the sons of God."[25] Some things are for children, some others are for mature sons and daughters. There are awesome resources that God is set to deliver, but they are for mature sons and daughters. Who will put you in charge of the whole store if you have not been faithful over the few things? God wants to put some people in charge of the store. I want to keep the store. I am not fighting for survival anymore; I want to be a manager of God's resources.

Receive grace to overcome every limitation imposed on you until now. Where others failed, you will succeed. Whatever stopped others will not be able to stop you. The spirit of poverty, lack, and wastage will not be able to catch up with you anymore.

Chapter Seven

Starting a Business

The most powerful resource in the world is revelation. That is why there is a powerful connection between the prophetic and your prosperity. There will always be resources around you; and the prophetic anointing helps to open your eyes to discover them. With the recognition of the resources at your disposal, you can have something to take to the market to exchange for cash. When Jehoshaphat the king realized that, he said, "Believe in the Lord your God, and you shall be established; believe His prophets, and you shall prosper."[1] Elisha the prophet looked at a widow and said, "What do you have in the house?" She said, "Nothing, but a jar of oil." He said, "Go, borrow vessels from everywhere, from all your neighbors—empty vessels; do not gather just a few. And when you have come in, you shall shut the door behind you and your sons; then pour it into all those vessels, and set aside the full ones."[2] And when she obeyed the prophet, intangible resources were converted to tangible resources for her, and she got something with which to start a business.

Businesses, to a large extent, build the economy of a nation. People who have the capacity to start and run businesses create jobs, goods and services, and opportunities for government to earn taxes and foreign exchange. In my part of the world, Nigeria, people's perception of business has to change. The average citizen thinks doing business is essentially patronizing government officials for contracts. This is because it is government that controls most of the money from oil. So unless there is a release of budgetary allocation from the government, everybody is stranded, literally speaking. That structure is changing now, because doing business simply requires us to identify people's needs and create and/or sell products and services to meet those needs at a modest profit.

There are many countries in the world where there is a favorable environment for starting and running businesses, but because people in many parts of Africa have been programmed to get a good education and then to get a good and secure job, many are afraid to launch out into business. But God will open our eyes to the opportunities available to us. And as we take bold steps in faith, there will be a season of transfer of wealth—the kind that happened in Egypt.[3]

BUSINESS WITH A NEW STRUCTURE

Economic structures are changing. God is about to raise individuals in His Kingdom who will be wealthier than some governments. I pray that will be the lot of people who read this book. It will manifest because of the blessing of Abraham that is on your life. Your business and value will give you influence over cities and nations. When you visit another country, you will be given diplomatic reception because you will be a guest not just of a business organization, but of the government itself. To those in the developing parts of the world, I know that we confront corrupt systems sometimes. But anyone who depends on the corrupt system for survival cannot change such a system. God is raising people through His power. Whereas the limitations in the environment are beginning to stop some people—this group of people I am referring to cannot be stopped.

Laban employed his nephew, Jacob, and found out that Jacob had an anointing that made him prosperous. Jacob said, "Send me away, that I may go to my own place and to my country." Laban said; "Please stay, if I have found favor in your eyes, for I have learned by experience that the Lord has blessed me for your sake." Jacob was critical to Laban's business success.[4]

Some people ask me why I think everybody should learn how to start and run a business. I say, even if you do not want to start an organization, you must have the mindset of an entrepreneur to rise to the highest level. This is because whoever started the organization in which you work was first an entrepreneur, except if you are in the civil service. When you can think like the business owner, creating innovative solutions, you will come to the attention of top management quickly. Sometimes, you can go as far as to invent new divisions of the business that become the future of the business. Joseph worked for Potiphar, and the Bible says that God blessed Potiphar for Joseph's sake. Potiphar himself saw that whatever Joseph did prospered, because the Lord was with him.[5]

When a person has intangible wealth in the spirit realm, that person brings wealth to an organization. Although Joseph was supposed to be a slave, his mindset broke that limit because he was an entrepreneur. He had the capacity to invent wealth. This is what God's Word says, that God has given us the power to produce or invent wealth. So where other people will be stranded, we will not because we can see what their eyes cannot see and hear what their ears cannot hear. We can see wealth in the desert while they see poverty and difficulty. We can see a forest in the wilderness because we have access to a realm to which other people do not have access.

> *Eye has not seen, nor ear heard, nor have entered into the heart of man the things which God has prepared for those*

who love Him. But God has revealed them to us through His Spirit....[6]

So Potiphar's business was doing well. Joseph was supposed to be a slave in his house, but Potiphar changed his title. He put everything under Joseph's supervision. Every reasonable boss would want to do that. Then something happened; Potiphar's wife lied against Joseph and he landed in jail. However, though he was supposed to be a prisoner, his mindset was bigger than the prison. Joseph was thinking of how to improve the way the prison was run. By the time he gave one or two proposals to the prison warden, the man changed the job description of his staff to allow Joseph to run the prison. This is because he came in with the mindset of a manager and leader. I describe it as the mindset of an entrepreneur.

Get ready, I believe that believers will take over the running of sports clubs very soon. Please note, the people who make the most money in sports are not the athletes, they are the owners of the clubs. While the average athlete has raw talent and skill, the person with organizational ability makes most of the money. Business is the ability to organize systems for the production, distribution, and consumption of goods and services. That is what makes the difference. That is what Joseph had; it is what Jacob had that Esau did not have.

That is one thing the developed parts of the world have that many developing nations do not have—the ability to build systems and to grow the people who run them. Eventually Joseph was sent for in the palace. With his entrepreneurial mindset, he organized Egypt; and during a global economic recession, Egypt exploded with wealth because there was an anointed man in the cabinet.[7]

There is a proverb that says, "The rich rules over the poor, and the borrower is servant to the lender."[8] But that first line is what has been ringing in my spirit. When you want to organize the systems in the nation, especially the political system, bear that in mind. The rich, even if their money is stolen, rule over the poor. I believe that God is giving us the power to create wealth, so we can influence every sphere of life in our nations, regions, and communities, and establish the values of the Kingdom of God.

RULING BY REVELATION

When God wants to create a shift, He brings on the scene professionals and entrepreneurs who will change the landscape. The anointing that God is giving us now is the anointing that has the capacity to displace principalities.

> *Then the Lord showed me four craftsmen. And I said, "What are these coming to do?" So he said, "These are the horns that scattered Judah, so that no one could lift up his head; but the craftsmen are coming to terrify them, to cast out the horns of the nations that lifted up their horn against the land of Judah to scatter it."* [9]

There was a time when some worldwide used to say, "If only Christians were in government, things would change." People have stopped saying that because countries saw some Christians go into government, and some of them succumbed to the temptation of corruption. Anyone who wants to function in a strategic leadership position must begin to appreciate that he or she will have to deal with principalities and powers, rulers of the darkness of this world and wicked spirits in heavenly realms. They will be superintending over a territory where satan has laid claim. There are positions that when occupied, people can become possessed if they do not carry an apostolic anointing, which gives them the capacity to displace principalities and powers.

Don't go into leadership in government or business if you have not emptied yourself of the potential for selfishness. Don't do it if you have not come to the same point Jesus came to after not eating for forty days. He had the power to turn a stone into bread. Satan said, "Use Your power." When you have desperate financial needs and God puts within your reach things that you do not have the right to take, if you have not yet come to the point where your head and your spirit can still be clear enough to put revelation first, do not move near leadership.

That is the essence of this book—revelation. What put Jesus above that temptation was revelation. He said, "It is written, 'Man shall not live by bread alone.'"[10] Christ's definition of success was different from the general belief that measures success by the acquisition of material possessions. His definition of power was different. It did not have to do with position. Neither did it have to do with acquisition. Until you come to the point that you do not define success by the size of your house, the kind of clothes you put on, or by the kind of obeisance that people show to you, don't desire to handle more money or power.

Thank God we now know like Jesus did, that even when we do not have a loaf of bread, we can still be rich because of our access to spiritual resources. "Silver and gold I do not have, but what I do have I give you."[11] Please read this book over and over until you catch the revelation—until the seeds fall into your heart and produce fruit. "And you shall know the truth, and the truth shall make you free."[12] By the truth that wealth is not only material, you are free from the spirit of poverty. This means you are free from the deceptions and desperation that drive the majority of people in our world today. You are free from societal pressure.

This is a prophetic season. The sons and daughters of God are coming to scatter the horns that have held people in bondage on a global dimension.

STEPS TO STARTING A BUSINESS

First of all, get rid of the fear of starting a business. It is only normal for us to feel inadequate when we are about to tread in unfamiliar terrain. When God moves you from Egypt and you are about to enter Canaan, you must understand that He is not dependent solely or entirely on your experience or intelligence; He is about to give you miracles, and what He requires from you is faith. Moses said:

> *Hear, O Israel: you are to cross over the Jordan today, and go in to dispossess nations greater and mightier than yourself, cities great and fortified up to heaven, a people great and tall, the descendants of the Anakim, whom you know, and of whom you heard it said, who can stand before the descendants of Anak.*[13]

So the way for us to possess territories in the business world is by faith. Otherwise, we may be intimidated. If the business terrain is new to you, then boldly declare to yourself, *I am about to possess a line of business that is bigger than I am. I am about to control sums of money that are greater than I have ever seen. It is coming to pass.*

If you want to start a business, first find a business to start. Remember, a business is just a system for production, distribution, and consumption of goods and services. Develop the skills for identifying people's needs. Find out what people need around you. A few centuries ago, business was not so complex, when the global economy was mainly based on agriculture. Every family owned its own farm. Then somewhere along the line, people invented corporations to limit their liability and to give them leverage because the scope of production was beginning to explode, especially during the industrial revolution.

When starting a business, take the complexity away from your mind. It is as simple as you discovering what people need, and it could be as simple as selling water, food, candlesticks, shoes, or providing transportation.

In many countries today, the system of education was designed decades ago to support the industrial revolution. It was designed to produce employees en-mass to work in the large industries and factories that evolved during this period. This is unfortunate for us now because there is no industrial revolution in most countries. Let us come back to the basics. The challenge we now have is that students graduating from the school system have the erroneous thought, *I need to work for somebody. I need to find an industry or an organization for which to work.* However, there are basic needs in every community that must be met. For example, in my country, meeting basic needs have been left to people who do not have much education. The people who are best equipped to invent and innovate to meet those basic needs have their heads in the air looking for someone to employ them. So it is the people whose minds have not been shaped by formal education, who have their minds free enough to identify those basic needs and meet them—they are the ones who are willing to sell basic things. And some of them are making more money than those who have a higher education—those who are looking for jobs that do not exist.

I live in a country where a powerful market is waiting to be awakened. With a population of about 150 million people who have basic needs that must be met on a daily basis, the prospects for business are exciting. Unfortunately, the prevailing economic structure despises the potential of the large population and goes after the money coming from just one resource—oil. But I declare in Jesus' name that the structure has changed. Soon, money made from the businesses generated by the needs of the 150 million people will overtake the money made from oil.

Therefore, those who are entrepreneurs need only to look around to spot people's basic needs and begin to meet those needs. Identify the needs that fit your gifts, skills, and values. You are already wired to meet certain needs. Find them. Be willing to start small. I know that some individuals make very large amounts of money from single contracts from the government, but it doesn't work like that for everybody. Well, if you start small and keep at it, you can grow to earn millions and billions. Also, the contracts from government will always be there, but they will become a very small part of the economy very soon. Don't be in a hurry.

In the developed parts of the world, people may wonder what products or services they can provide that have not already been rendered. You need to remind yourself that though the methods of presentation may change, the basic needs of humankind remain the same. People will always need to eat, drink, sit, sleep, learn, move around, be sheltered, and be clothed. They will need peace, love, and happiness. How they are produced, packaged, and presented will change, but then you should remind yourself that innovation is an endless thing. Nothing is in its perfect state of development yet.

MAKE IMPROVEMENTS

When finding a business to start, there is a convenient way to approach it; look at existing products and services and simply improve them. That is the basic way to start. Ask questions about existing products and services because most of people's needs are already being met one way or the other. Improve the processes by which those needs are being met or improve those products and services themselves. It can make starting a business cheap.

I bought some shirts from a member of our church. She resigned from her job at a bank and began to make shirts. The first time she showed me the shirts that her company produced, I was surprised. I was surprised because they were of high quality and her designs are exceptional. She imports the fabrics and then makes beautiful shirts and skirts. I was also impressed by the branding and packaging; she obviously received professional input, because the name, colors, and font sizes are attractive. So I patronize her business because I need a lot of shirts for my television broadcasts. She is meeting the basic need for clothing and improved the way it is done in her environment. I had previously tried some other locally produced shirts, but they were of poor quality. What she did is not rocket science. She simply improved the quality of the product. That is one of the ways to find a business to start. Take a good look at the products and services that are being offered around you and improve the quality and/or the way they are being offered.

To succeed and to continue to succeed in business, you must develop the ability to innovate. With this quality, all the problems people have around you become your opportunities. I see huge opportunities in my environment. For example, I like to eat fresh corn. Some call it corn on the cob. We cook it in our home when it is in season, but we don't always have time to make it. Some sell it along the road, but that isn't always an option for me these days. For instance, one day my wife and I stopped along the road by a lady who was cooking and selling corn. As I rolled down the car window, her eyes lit up. She shouted, "Hey, this is the man who teaches me on television!" Although I was happy to hear of the impact our broadcast made in her life, I wasn't excited about the possibility of people crowding around. Gratefully, the people around did not hear her.

Actually, I prefer to go into a clean store to see fresh corn prepared and sold. In some parts of the world, I have bought corn on the cob, sweet, hot, and layered with butter. Millions of people eat fresh corn in my country every year, and I believe that there are many who would like their corn to be prepared more creatively and more hygienically. Because they desire better quality service, they will not mind paying more. Furthermore, corn grows during the rainy season, so people don't have corn to eat during the dry season. Someone could find ways to preserve it and sell it during the dry season even though it may cost a bit more then. Well, I have some good news. In the course of writing this book, I visited a new supermarket in my neighborhood and saw a kiosk where they sell sweet corn. I said, "Bravo." Finally somebody is getting the concept of providing people what they want and need.

What I have tried to do with the illustration of the corn is to show that basic human needs give us the opportunity to do business if we can identify people's needs and if we are innovative. There are many products and services that the Holy Spirit is going to open up to us during this season. You will find your area of impact. Whatever is called a problem around you has become an opportunity for you. Find a business to start. Identify people's needs; that is the greatest clue to look for.

Now, one of the easy ways to identify people's needs is for you to look at your own needs. You need food, and others need food too. You need water, that is proof others also need water. And because you need a house to live in, everybody else does, too. The important point is this; do not just be a consumer, be the one providing the products or services. Even if you are still a student, I encourage you to open your eyes. Every student in your school or in your class has the same needs that you have. You need textbooks, they also need textbooks. You need notebooks, so they need notebooks. You need pens, erasers, pencils, and other such items. All the students in your class also need them. Come to the classroom and be a problem solver. Be the one selling the things they need to buy. Just to stretch it a bit further, if you are a guy, you certainly need haircuts. Then all the guys in your dormitory, neighborhood, and town need haircuts.

I look back over my time as a student and I laugh at my level of ignorance of money matters then. When we had someone who was smart enough to sell things on the campus, we called them names. There was a young man who organized film shows. He would write advertisements for the films on cardboard paper and post them around the campus. Ultimately, he made money from other students in exchange for the entertainment that he provided. Well, your friends may tease you. They may even call you names, but you go ahead anyway—be the one providing products and services. Find a business to start, and where you are now will be a rehearsal for the next level.

RESEARCH AND EVALUATE YOUR IDEAS

In preparation to start a business, you need to do some research. You need to work with practical facts though you are being led by revelation. Revelation will show you where you are going and probably what to do. But you have to start from where you are. Deal with things the way they are. Go around and ask questions:

- Do people really need what you want to offer?

- What specific problem is your product or service going to solve? That question touches the heart of everything.

- Who will buy your product or service? Will it be predominantly men, women, students, youth, or older people? Will it be professional or business people?

- Why will they buy your product or service?

- Where will they buy your product or service? They will buy some things in shops, and some prefer to buy online. Some they will buy in hairdressing salons. Knowing where people will most likely buy a product or service will help you know where to position your product or service. People must be made aware that your product or service exists—position them for high visibility.

- What do I need to charge to make a healthy profit? Pricing can be very technical.

- Will people be willing to pay that amount of money? Sometimes, after you have figured all your calculations, you will abandon a business altogether when you see that the price of your product or service will discourage them from buying. Or you may have to rework some details and restructure your product completely depending on the affordability of what you are offering.

- Will people be willing to pay for the product or service?
- What products or services will yours be competing with?

You have to get to the root of these questions and answers. Even as a minister, I have found entrepreneurial thinking very helpful. When you read the story of Israel's movement from Egypt to Canaan, you realize that you need the mindset of an entrepreneur to take over Canaan. In Canaan you are not a slave; you are not working for somebody; you work for yourself. In Canaan, you have to be productive. The raw materials are there, but you have to be able to create wealth. Israel struggled with confidence when they got to the border of Canaan. They could not break free from the mindset of slavery. They were not creative. They didn't have the capacity to dream and to shape their world using sanctified imagination.

For God's people to be able to take the systems in our world today and establish the values of the Kingdom of God, we must be innovative. The world around us is evolving. If we are no longer relevant with respect to our message and systems, the world will seek leadership from other places. Pastors and church leaders must ask the same questions: What do people need? Who can we best reach? What kind of music do they listen to? What is competing with God in their lives? Why don't they come to church? And so on.

I remember the day I announced to our church that we would remodel the warehouse we had moved into a year before. We were going to put tiles on the floor, paint the whole place, install suspended ceilings, spotlights, and air conditioners. This was after we had asked some hard questions at a pastors' meeting. I had visited a restaurant not far from our church that was attracting a large patronage. As I sat there, I asked myself, *Why are all these people coming here? They are the same people I want to get into the church to worship God.* I made some observations, the core of which had to do with the quality and presentation of their food. It was not long after that, that the Lord gave me marching orders on the renovation work we should carry out in church.

After my announcement, some people asked the church administrator after the service why the church was going to waste so much money on improving a rented building. I found out that it was some businesspeople in church who were asking those questions. At that time, it was not as common in my city to have church facilities look beautiful and have air conditioning like we have now. So I asked the church administrator, "Have you been to their stores and offices? Have you seen how beautiful their places of business are? If they think that is okay for their businesses, and almost all of them are in rented buildings, why do they think it is too much for the house of God to look good?"

Really, it's not that they were bad people. They were well-meaning people. But they were not used to seeing a church look beautiful. We did the renovation. We broke into two services a week before we turned on the air conditioning. In less than two months, the two services were full, and we had to begin preparations for the third one. We created a new level entirely for our ministry. And this is the essence of my story—look for ways to improve what is being done or the way it is being done, and you will have a profitable business and even take over many of the businesses around.

Do you have a vision to own an airline or a manufacturing company? Nothing is difficult for God. They will soon come looking for you because of your work and vision. How much lobbying did Joseph do on his own behalf before they invited him to the palace? None. So do not think it is going to be difficult. The things that are impossible with people are possible with God. Get ready to unleash God's kind of creativity to solve problems nationally and globally.

CALCULATE YOUR COST

The next step toward starting a business is to calculate everything it will cost to take off. You have to be very practical and realistic. Factor in all the money you will need until the business breaks even. Many young businesses fail because human nature tempts their owners to overestimate the profits they will earn and to underestimate how much they need to spend until they break even. So they are stranded midway. That brings to mind again what Jesus said:

> *For which of you, intending to build a tower, does not sit down first and count the cost, whether he has enough to finish it—lest, after he has laid the foundation, and is not able to finish, all who see it begin to mock him.*[14]

I pray that your vision will not be aborted, and you will not be mocked. Do your homework well.

WRITE A BUSINESS PLAN

A business plan is a working document that serves as a road map for your business. With it you state the steps you will take to move your business from dream to reality. It compels you to think and clarify your goals. It helps you to prioritize when making decisions. And it becomes the basis for measuring success for you and your employees. A business plan is also a marketing tool with which you persuade banks or investors to put their funds in the business. It helps you to foresee possible problems and to create strategies for preventing or managing them.

State the name of the business on the cover. Have a table of contents that lists: Vision; Operational Plan; Marketing Plan;

Financial Plan. State the vision of the business; for example: "To become the number one provider of innovative online payment services in Europe." After that, write a chapter each on your *operational plan*, marketing plan, and financial plan. Your operational plan should include your assumptions; these are from the answers to those questions you asked in your survey. The survey must have helped you spot a market gap, which will help you identify your unique selling proposition. Your *marketing plan* should identify the people who are going to buy your goods or services and why they are going to buy yours. It should identify the products you are competing against, and state how your product is different from the others. And then write your *financial plan*. Calculate your projection for sales and profits for the first year and for the first three years. Estimate your projection for expenditures, too. But please be very realistic.

Remember, what you are building is transgenerational, so do not put yourself under pressure to become a billionaire in one year. Increase will come in cycles and because you are acting on revelation, it is inevitable. Be patient. Give yourself time to breakeven and do not put yourself under pressure, especially in the first year.

IDENTIFY SOURCES OF FINANCING

From where will you get your start-up funds? Many get stuck over the issue of capital, but it should not be as confusing as it seems. There are various possible ways to source funds. First is your savings. Your ability to keep aside part of your income consistently says a lot about your ability to manage money. That aspect of your character also gives confidence to potential investors. If you have been working at a job for five years or more, and you do not have any savings, a smart investor will easily see that you will do to his or her money what you have done with yours. Having your savings for capital becomes a huge advantage if you live in an environment where there isn't easy access to credit.

You may also ask for money from your friends and relations. But as much as possible, avoid loans from family or friends. If things go wrong, precious relationships can be destroyed. In any case, trust God to be the One in the position to give loans. "You shall lend to many nations, but you shall not borrow."[15] Also, "The wicked borrows and does not repay, but the righteous shows mercy and gives."[16] If you ever leverage on credit, let it be your highest priority to pay back the money as fast as possible. Most times, funds from friends and family are gifts or interest free loans. The only requirement is credibility with your friends and relations. If you borrowed money before and you did not return it, you will have to go elsewhere. I have heard many people complain that their rich relations are very stingy. What they don't say is that they received money from such people before, but mismanaged it and didn't repay it. They closed the door on themselves.

You can also generate cash from your assets. You can sell your vehicle, electronics, jewelry, land, building, or stocks to raise cash. When the business gets going and you have made money, you can replace your asset. If your esteem is not tied to material things, you will be able to do this so you can move on to a higher level financially. A woman once approached her pastor to ask for financial help. She was lamenting that she did not have money to start a business. He just looked at her and said, "I can see the money on you. You have money." She said, "No, I do not have the money, sir. If I had the money, I would not come to you." He said, "But I can see it. It's in that gold chain around your neck. Sell it." A lady heard me on the radio say that there will always be something around you that God can use to move you to the next level financially. She then sold bottles to raise enough cash for transportation to see an uncle who gave her money to start a business. Trust that God will open your eyes to see the assets that hold your start-up capital.

You can raise funds from your suppliers. This is one of the cheapest sources of funds. For example, if you want to sell books and you find a distributor who has his warehouse full of books, you can negotiate to take some of the books on credit, and to return the money at an agreed date. Such transactions happen infrequently, but you never know what you can do until you try. Life does not give you what you deserve but what you demand. When you ask you receive. Remember, there is a connection between money and faith. You must believe there is a way for you to start, and God will show you the way. What you need to raise capital this way is integrity. This is where you realize that integrity is as good as cash. To succeed in the long term, you must keep your promises. Pay the supplier before or on the agreed date. You will enjoy even better favor in the future. If for reasons you cannot control you are unable to pay on the agreed date, call before the deadline expires to explain why. Don't avoid the person. Remember, you have an unusual opportunity to use your supplier's funds to do business. Don't blow your chance. Keep your promises.

Also, you can raise funds from the bank. That is why banks exist, to give leverage so people can use resources beyond their current ability to take advantage of unusual opportunities. But this purpose has been abused because of greed. Many take loans not to create wealth but to fund their lust for material things. Some banks too would rather give credit to fund consumption, not investment. To finance your ideas from the bank, you must have developed sophisticated financial management ability, and you must be highly disciplined. To be candid, with the kind of high interest rates in my environment, I advise people who do not have business experience to avoid such loans. In the first place, they usually do not understand the bank's terms. They can't read the fine print. In fact, in such transactions, the things that are not written are as important as the things that are written. When things go wrong, I see the anxiety, fear, and anguish that people go through, all because of their lack of experience.

Now, let me tell you what I have heard some rich people say, "The best time to take a loan is when you can do without it." In other words, you take it only because you don't want to touch your wealth to start a new venture.

BEGIN THE START-UP PROCESS

Begin your start-up legal work. Talk to a lawyer or a certified public accountant and register your business. You will have to decide whether it is a sole proprietorship—you are the sole owner of the business if it will be a limited liability company, or a partnership. The structure of the business determines how it will be registered.

Advertise. The next step is to advertise. Let people know that you exist. Let them know what you have to offer, what makes it different, and where they can get it. There is a common saying that the person who refuses to advertise is like a man who winks at a girl in the dark. He knows what he is doing but the girl does not. Now you don't have to go on television and spend money that you don't have. Leverage first on cheap or free publicity. Make contact with presenters of programs on television or radio, or with newspaper reporters, and let them know that you have something to say. They need people who speak passionately and intelligently about their subjects to attract people to their programs or newspapers.

Also, seek ways to get directly in touch with the people you have identified as your targets. Inform the exact people you want to patronize your business. Be very creative and innovative about it. "Nor do they light a lamp and put it under a basket, but on a lampstand, and it gives light to all who are in the house."[17]

Begin! The thing to do now is to start. Some people have done everything we have talked about up until this point. The only thing they have not done is start. If you want everything to be perfect before you start, you will never start. "He who waits for perfect conditions will never get anything done."[18] The reason why many people fail at this point is because it requires courage, and most people do not have courage. Their lives are ruled by fear and self-doubt. They look at someone who has tried and is doing well as a spectacular person. Successful people are exactly like you. God is no respecter of persons. The only difference is that they were courageous enough to have tried. You never know what you can do until you attempt it. I have more respect for the person who tries and fails than for the person who has never tried or failed. The best way to avoid failure is to do nothing. The person who tries and fails is closer to the answer than the person who has not tried at all.

If you want to succeed in business, make failure a learning experience. I have met people in some cultures where there is strong belief in sorcery and witchcraft. Their lives are ruled by fear. Once something does not go right, they quickly blame it on the enemies. If it is enemies that do not allow things to work out the first time, then all of us have enemies. There is no guarantee things will always work out the first time. It is not a perfect world. Now, it is not that I don't believe that witches exist, but it's ridiculous for a Christian to name them as an excuse for failure. We have authority in Christ to tread over serpents and scorpions and over all the power of the enemy, and nothing shall by any means hurt us.[19] Knowing that, we can persist until we get the material equivalent of what God has given us by revelation.

Even in prayer, Jesus taught us that we should learn to pray with persistence. The illustration He used was that of a man who went to his friend in the middle of the night because he had a guest but did not have food at home. He asked his friend for food, but his friend refused him. His excuse was that he was already in bed with his kids and did not want to touch dirt again. But the man who needed bread stayed there and continued to knock. When his friend saw that both of them were not going to sleep, he got up and gave him the bread.[20] Jesus explained that the one man gave the bread to the other, not because they were friends, but because of the other man's persistence. Jesus was teaching that even in prayer, persistence is needed.

Elijah prayed seven times on Mount Carmel before rain fell.[21] Israel went around Jericho seven days, and on the seventh day, seven times.[22] Naaman went into the river seven times before his skin was healed.[23] If you try something and it doesn't work, try it again. Just change your approach a little bit. I have lost the fear of starting. I found out things are not always as bad as they seem. I can imagine someone who has been organizing seminars. If that is all the person has been doing the past five years, by now he or she must have become an expert on how to plan and organize seminars. People don't attend seminars when they are still at the idea stage. They attend the ones that are happening live. So, go ahead. Organize!

When my wife, Nike, wanted to start a seminar for women, we discussed it and agreed she should give it a try. She decided to use a small hall that could seat about sixty to seventy people. She informed people about the topic and where it would be held. When the day of the seminar came, the place was packed full. In fact, some people could not get in. Wow! Take note, you don't have to tell those who ask the exact number of people who were at your first seminar. Tell them the place was so packed many people couldn't find seats. An African proverb says, "The lizard that fell from the Iroko (a very tall tree in Nigeria) tree and nods its head is simply saying, 'If nobody will congratulate me, I will congratulate myself.'" Even God looked at what He had created at the end of each day in Genesis, and said it was good. Celebrate small wins. Over time, your efforts will compound to deliver great results. By the way, someone who attended Nike's first seminar suggested to her a few days later that she should run the next seminar at one of the most prestigious hotels in the city—and this lady paid for the use of the hotel.

You just don't know the miracles that are waiting for you until you start. Nobody will fund your hesitation. They will fund what they see working. You will be surprised at the resources and opportunities that will come to you when people see you doing something. So, Nike had the second seminar in the banquet hall of the hotel. It could seat about 350 people. Those who showed up that day were almost double the capacity of the hall.

I have a feeling some people's miracles have been waiting for four, five, or six years while they have been planning to do business. In our world, people don't recognize or reward you for what you are *planning* to do, but for what you have done. I have yet to meet the person who was awarded a Ph.D. for planning to study mechanical engineering. As you make the bold move, blessings shall come upon you and overtake you. When you act on revelation, you commit God to act on your behalf.

Moses said:

> *Now it shall come to pass, **if you diligently obey the voice of the Lord your God**, to observe carefully all His commandments which I command you today, that the Lord your God will set you high above all nations of the earth. And all these **blessings shall come upon you** and overtake you, because you obey the voice of the Lord your God: Blessed shall you be in the city, and blessed shall you be in the country. Blessed shall be the fruit of your body, the produce of your ground and the increase of your herds, the increase of your cattle and the offspring of your flocks. Blessed shall be your basket and your kneading bowl. Blessed shall you be when you come in, and blessed shall you be when you go out.*[24]

Amen!

Chapter Eight

Financial Freedom

You become financially free when the returns on your investment can pay your bills.

I will share two dimensions to financial freedom: If my monthly expenses total $1,000, and I have money in the bank, say in a certificate of deposit (CD), and the interest that I am getting from the CD is $1,500 every month, the implication is that all my bills will be paid, even if I do not work again. That is one of the most important manifestations of financial freedom. To reemphasize, we are rich and financially free already in Christ. Now we are working toward the physical manifestation of our wealth.

Many people aim too low when they set their financial goals. They aim for financial security; and their definition of financial security is to have a job and to be sure that nothing is going to take that job away. Seeing the effects of the global economic recession, it is obvious that there may not really be security in job security. My position is that we should not aim for security; rather we should aim for financial freedom, which is being in a state where we don't have to worry about money.

First we should connect with God until we get the revelation, or spiritual wealth, that defines our financial status. Then we should take practical steps to manifest our freedom.

Plan to change the way you work as you grow older. If your goal is to get to that point where the returns on your investment can pay your bills—the point at which you do not have to work for money anymore—you can now work for fulfillment. You work for joy and for significance, which you get by adding value to people's lives. That should be a goal for all of us. It is a goal that I encourage you to set for the long term. This goal should be for twenty, forty, or sixty years ahead, and the sooner you start the better for you. When you have such a long term goal, then compound interest will work for you.

APPLYING THE LAW OF COMPOUND INTEREST

Urban legend says that Albert Einstein[1] said that compound interest is the most powerful force of the universe. The fact that you can invest with interest and then you can take the capital plus the interest and invest that again is awesome. When you do that over and over again, somewhere along the line, the numbers explode geometrically. The longer the number of years you invest, the better it works for you. I have an example. If you invest $1,000 per year for the next thirty years, your total investment will be $30,000. If you get very good returns of 12 percent per annum on your investment and you do not make any withdraws, in thirty years, your money would have grown to $270,294.50.

Look at the difference. You have invested just $30,000, but your money has grown to more than $270,000. Likewise, if you invest $10,000 a year for thirty years, you will invest a total of $300,000, but your money will grow to over $2,700,000. There are so many people who can afford to invest at least a hundred dollars a month, but they don't. For some, it is because they are ignorant of the principles with which wealth is created. Second, to prosper this way demands discipline and consistency.

"The thoughts of the [steadily] diligent tend only to plenteousness, but everyone who is impatient and hasty hastens only to want."[2] Some people start out well after reading a book like this. They develop a spending plan and try to control their spending. But after a month or two, it becomes too much of a burden and they forget about it. Then they look for another fast-working formula for financial breakthrough. They may begin to jump from one breakthrough anointing service to the other; and nothing is wrong with attending an anointing service, but they cannot substitute that with the discipline of doing the Word on a consistent basis. Some even fall prey to get-rich-quick schemes, but we know they almost always cause people to get *poor* quick.

Being rich is a habit, and being poor is a habit. Be consistent in daily prayer and meditation in the Word so you can access spiritual wealth. Have a plan, and do something every day that will move you closer to your goals.

How to Invest

In recent times, the global economy has been so unstable that people's confidence in financial markets has been terribly shaken. Many who invested in stocks have had their monies wiped out and some are now in serious debt. But you know what? Circumstances may change, but principles never change. If you make the mistake of responding or reacting to circumstances which are temporary, you may shortchange yourself in the long run. If you read the history of investing, you will see that recessions come, once in a long while. It is just part of the cycle.

There was famine in the time of Abraham, also in the time of Isaac. And there was a global famine in the days of Jacob and Joseph. In the vision that Pharaoh had that Joseph interpreted, there were seven years of plenty and seven years of dryness.[3] But do not think that those events stopped then; it is a cycle. People who invest know that the best way to invest is to invest for the long term. Invest for twenty or thirty years, or longer. Just continue to make that monthly investment. Do not mind the circumstances. If the markets go down, they will come up again.

Ultimately, if you continue to invest over a few decades, you will prosper. The investments will pay you in the long run. So I want to encourage those of us who may have been burnt because we made some risky investments—we should continue to save and invest in fixed-interest deposits, stocks, real estate, and other investment instruments. But please remember that you need professional advice from the experts before you make any investments.

Talking about risky investments, when some of these funny investment schemes came up that were multiplying people's money over sixty days, I remember that I warned our church members about get-rich-quick schemes. I told them what I read from Dr. Robert Allen's book, *Multiple Streams of Income*,[4] that you should split your investment money into three groups. He says that people should invest 50 percent of savings in investments that yield about 20 percent increment per annum. They are not very high yielding and the results are not dramatic. In other words, you should be conservative in your investment. No one can afford to work hard, save money, and then watch it blow away. God's Word says:

> *I have seen real misery here on earth: money saved is a curse to its owners. They lose it all in a bad deal and have nothing to give to their children. People come into this world with nothing, and when they die they leave with nothing. In spite of all their hard work, they leave just as they came.*[5]

Robert Allen also says another 30 percent of our investment money should be put in investments that yield between 50 to

100 percent increment per annum. Then he says we should invest the last 20 percent of our savings in investments that yield over 100 percent per annum. He further says we must erect concrete walls between those three categories. In other words, if you blow your money in one category, do not reach over to the other category to take money for investing. When people record losses in their investments, they sometimes become desperate to recover, and have a tendency to do some desperate investing. It is better to cut your losses early. And don't forget, greed is a weakness of human nature. Don't give in to greed.

THE SPIRITUAL EXCHANGE

There is a superior kind of investment, and I want to close with the spiritual exchange. In this investment, you take your money and your material wealth and you exchange it for intangible wealth. Hear again what Jesus said:

> *Do not lay up for yourselves treasures on earth, where moth and rust destroy and where thieves break in and steal; but lay up for yourselves treasures in heaven, where neither moth nor rust destroys and where thieves do not break in and steal. For where your treasure is, there your heart will be also.* [6]

Jesus was saying that you can build up material wealth and investment, but you can also build up intangible wealth. The problem with material wealth is that it can be wiped out in one day. Solomon said, "Do not overwork to be rich."[7] And that is because riches can develop wings and fly away. Material wealth can be wiped out within a short time. Jesus said you can build up intangible wealth that thieves can never steal. And when you know the process for changing intangible wealth to tangible wealth, then you can always reach into the spiritual realm to convert your wealth into its material equivalent.

If you read through the Gospels, you will realize that this was the kind of wealth that Jesus had. He was the wealthiest person walking the earth when He was around; but it was not because He had the largest amount of money in the account. It was because He had access to get whatever He needed, whenever He needed it. He got five loaves of bread and two fish from a young boy, and He fed a crowd of some fifteen to twenty thousand people. That is wealth. And for us as Christians, Jesus gives us a redefinition for prosperity.

With the Jesus definition of prosperity, I can today stand in the presence of the person who stole millions and have self-esteem, because there is a difference between success as a person and success as an event. If you steal or defraud people to be prosperous, you may have achieved your goal, which we describe as success, but you are a fraud. In the new global economy, people with intangible wealth are going to be more prosperous than those who are stealing.

I believe real wealth is about to be rediscovered. In the Bible, those who laid the foundation for our faith discovered a way for investing in the intangible world. They discovered how to turn their tangible wealth into intangible wealth through the principle of exchange of value.

Abraham met Melchizedek the high priest of God. In Genesis 14:18-20, I believe we see that Melchizedek was the manifestation of Jesus in the Old Testament. In Hebrews 7, we read that Melchizedek had neither father nor mother. There was nobody like that. In this particular instance, Jesus met Abraham ahead of time. And He gave Abraham bread and wine, which were going to be the symbol of the blood covenant in the New Testament. This person then blessed him, and Abraham gave him tithes.[8] It was an exchange. Spiritual wealth is what we call blessing. It is intangible, it is invisible, but it is on your life. Talking about the blessing, Abraham had it, Isaac had it, and Jacob had it.

Let us use Jacob as an example again. He was with his brother Esau who was hungry. Jacob had food and used it to buy intangible wealth—Esau's birthright. The birthright was the right to inherit the father's blessing as the firstborn, which could not be activated until the father, Isaac, died. What Jacob got with a plate of food was the future. He bought intangible wealth. On the day that Isaac was to die, he called Esau and said, "I want you to run, kill some animal, and prepare some good food for me." Isaac, the father, had intangible wealth. He had the blessing of Abraham. And although there was famine back in that day, Isaac still sowed his crops, received a hundred fold and more, to the point where the Philistines began to envy him.[9] He was prosperous because he had intangible wealth to convert. The economic recession could not wipe away his wealth.

Now, Isaac was about to die, and he wanted to transfer that wealth, the blessing of Abraham, to his son. But he made a powerful statement; he said, "And make me savory food, such as I love, and bring it to me that I may eat, that my soul may bless you before I die."[10] Isaac asked his son to activate the law of exchange—to bring the material so he could give him intangible wealth in exchange.

The only thing is, Esau did not own the birthright anymore, because the day he ate the porridge, he had transferred it to Jacob. So he was a cheat who was trying to get what did not belong to him anymore. See, things work out according to principles. What you sow, you will reap—even if you think that God has forgotten. Somehow Jacob and Esau's mother got involved, and she whispered to Jacob to prepare the food and to receive the blessing. So Jacob quickly prepared food and brought it. And Isaac did bless him. Let me declare those blessings on you reading this book. This is going to be your testimony.

> *And he came near and kissed him; and he smelled the smell of his clothing, and blessed him and said: "Surely, the smell of my son is like the smell of a field which the LORD has blessed. Therefore may God give you of the dew of heaven, of the fatness of the earth, and plenty of grain and wine. Let peoples serve you, and nations bow down to you. Be master*

over your brethren, and let your mother's sons bow down to you. Cursed be everyone who curses you, and blessed be those who bless you!"[11]

That is it. Wealth transferred. As soon as Jacob left, Esau arrived. Then their father realized he had been deceived. Because he could no longer see, he shuddered as he told Esau that his brother had taken the blessing. You know what Esau did? The Bible says that he broke down and wept.[12]

My problem with our seemingly civilized generation is that we are blinded to the real things in life. Our values are misplaced. Esau was a man who had wives and children, and he wept, not because he lost a car or some money, but because he did not get the blessing. Intangible wealth is the real deal. Jacob exchanged the tangible for intangible. He used food to collect the real thing. You and I must invest in exchanging material wealth for intangible wealth so we can experience the incredible power of supernatural provision as people did in the Bible.

THE LAW OF GIVING

There is power in giving. When you are praying for prosperity, you must answer one question. Why do you want money? The answer is very important. If you do not understand the way money works, it will destroy you. Most people who ask for money do not know what they are asking for. "I want to be a millionaire," they say. Or "I want to be a billionaire." This is what comes with it. "Those who desire to be rich fall into temptation and a snare, and into many foolish and harmful lusts which drown men in destruction and perdition."[13] Is it wrong to be rich? No. But it depends on the purpose of our wealth.

The Bible tells of a man who prospered, yet had a problem with what he did or what he wanted to do with the wealth.[14] What is your relationship with money right now?

For the love of money is a root of all kinds of evil, for which some have strayed from the faith in their greediness, and pierced themselves through with many sorrows.[15]

Jesus said, "You cannot serve God and mammon."[16] You need to understand money before you get it. The only place money desires to take in your life is God's place. But God wants you to trust Him, for without faith, it is impossible to please God.[17]

The more money comes into your life, the more you are tempted to put your trust in the money. If you are not careful, you will not be able to trust God fully anymore. And once you put your security in money, you will not be able to afford to see the money go. At that point, greed will set in. Sometimes there are road signs: Speed Kills. Well, there is another sign I would like to post along the road: Greed Kills. I am serious. That is why Paul the apostle said, "Command those who are rich in this present age [those who have attained financial freedom] not to be haughty [wrestling with pride], *nor to trust in uncertain riches* but in the living God, who gives us richly all things to enjoy."[18]

DEALING WITH GREED

How do you break the hold of greed? You break it through giving. If you cannot give, you are under the control of money. You are not the one who has the money, the money has you. That is why God said:

> *"Bring all the tithes into the storehouse, that there may be food in My house, and try Me now in this," says the Lord of hosts, "If I will not open for you the windows of heaven, and pour out for you such blessing that there will not be room enough to receive it."*[19]

That is intangible wealth. Don't worry that for a start your tithe may be a small amount of money. God deals with proportions. It is not the quantity that impresses God, it is the proportion. Some argue over whether the tithe is a New Testament doctrine or not. Apart from the fact that it predates the Law of Moses, and Moses developed only variants of it, Jesus gave people instructions to give amounts that were more than the tithe. Consider the rich young ruler who Jesus told to sell everything and to distribute the money to the poor. It was going to take that action to free him from the spirit of greed.

Jesus sat down and watched the way people put money in the offering bag. Then He told His disciples, "Assuredly, I say to you that this poor widow has put in more than all those who have given to the treasury; for they all put in out of their abundance, but she out of her poverty put in all that she had, her whole livelihood."[20] The basic principle is established; revelation and greed don't work together. If you are generous, you will enjoy the flow of spiritual wealth.

Give to people in whose lives you see proof of grace that you desire in a specific area of your life. "Now beyond all contradiction the lesser is blessed by the better."[21] Give to your parents. "Honor your father and mother, which is the first commandment with promise: that it may be well with you and you may live long on the earth."[22] Also, give to ministers of the gospel because by the divine appointment of God, they carry the power of blessing; they carry intangible wealth.

If you want to exchange the material wealth that you have for the invisible one, God's servants are contact points for the release of the supernatural. When Saul and his father's servant were searching for their lost donkeys, they provoked the release of revelation by giving. "And the servant answered Saul again and said, "Look, I have here at hand one-fourth of a shekel of silver. I will give that to the man of God, to tell us our way."[23] One of the reasons why it would be difficult for me to entertain the thought of being poor is the amount of blessings that are released on my life through diverse kinds of giving.

I must warn that we must not give with wrong motives. There are impostors masquerading as ministers who give people the impression that they can buy the anointing just because they want to collect money from people. Their judgment is close by. The grace of God is not for sale. If you are a lover of money, don't bother to give. You are likely to hurt yourself. "But Peter said to him, 'Your money perish with you, because you thought that the gift of God could be purchased with money!'"[24]

GIVE TO THE POOR

Give to the poor. I love the blessings that God gives the person who gives to the poor.

> *Blessed is he who considers the poor; the Lord will deliver him in time of trouble. The Lord will preserve him and keep him alive, and he will be blessed on the earth; You will not deliver him to the will of his enemies. The Lord will strengthen him on his bed of illness; You will sustain him on his sickbed.*[25]

The person sustaining the life of the poor man must not die. "He who has pity on the poor lends to the Lord."[26] Each time you give to a poor person, it is a loan into the realm of the spirit, and God will pay you back. If you cannot give 10 percent of $1,000, you are certainly already under the grip of greed. If the richest people in the world like Bill Gates and Warren Buffet[27] have pledged to give a large proportion of their wealth away, they must have discovered something. There is a new wave of blessing that is coming; get ready to partake in it so you can establish God's dominion on the earth.

I pray that whatever stopped generations before now from claiming their real wealth will not stop you. I prophesy the release of wealth from Heaven, the kind that no generation has ever found before. I prophesy a new level of revelation in your life. I believe that the God who delivered me from the curse of poverty will lift you beyond every recession, depression, or stagnation.

I prophesy a season of miracles and supernatural provisions in your life. There are things God has reserved in the realm of the Spirit. He wants to release them now, and I present you to God as a candidate to take delivery of them.

You will not die; you will live to see the fulfillment of God's prophetic word in your life.

Endnotes

CHAPTER 1—YOU ARE WEALTHY

1. Russell H. Conwell, *Acres of Diamonds* (New York: Jove Books, 1986). First published in 1890 by the John Y. Huber Company, Philadelphia.

2. See Numbers 32:9-13.

3. Hebrews 4:1-2.

4. Hebrews 4:3a.

5. 2 Corinthians 8:9.

6. 2 Corinthians 5:21.

7. Mark 9:23b.

8. Matthew 4:9.

9. Luke 11:21-22.

10. Deuteronomy 8:18.

11. Mark 16:17a.

12. Jeremiah 33:3.
13. Mark 11:24.
14. Luke 24:32.
15. See Psalm 1:1-3.
16. 2 Chronicles 20:20.
17. See Genesis 14:18-20.
18. Proverbs 11:25.
19. Genesis 28:20-22.
20. Genesis 31:12-13a.
21. 1 Samuel 9:4.
22. See 1 Samuel 9:10,20.
23. See Luke 5:4-7.
24. 3 John 2.
25. Romans 12:2.
26. John 8:32.
27. See 2 Kings 5:8-14.
28. See Genesis 13:1-2.
29. See Genesis 26:12-14.
30. See Genesis 31.
31. See Mark 6:1-3.
32. Hebrews 11:3.
33. Genesis 1:2-3.
34. Genesis 1:26a KJV.

Endnotes

35. Genesis 1:28b KJV.
36. See Genesis 3.
37. Matthew 3:17b.
38. Matthew 4:4.
39. Matthew 6:31,33.
40. John 1:14.

CHAPTER 2—REDEFINING WEALTH

1. Proverbs 23:7.
2. Bill Gates III is an American business magnate, philanthropist, author and chairman of Microsoft, the computer software company he founded with Paul Allen. Gates' net worth in September 2011 was $59 billion. http://www.forbes.com/profile/bill-gates/; accessed October 3, 2011.
3. Proverbs 21:5.
4. 1 Corinthians 2:9-10.
5. Dr. Myles Munroe is the president and founder of the Bahamas Faith Ministries International, a Christian growth and resource center that includes leadership training institutes, a missions agency, a publishing company, a television network, radio and Web communications, and a church community.
6. Proverbs 22:1.
7. Matthew 16:26.
8. Genesis 25:29-34.
9. See Genesis 27.

10. Matthew 6:31,33.

11. Matthew 6:19-20.

12. Matthew 4:3.

13. Matthew 4:6a.

14. Matthew 4:9.

15. Genesis 14:18-20.

16. Malachi 3:10 paraphrased.

17. Genesis 14:21-23.

18. 2 Corinthians 8:9.

19. Galatians 2:20.

20. Acts 3:6 KJV.

21. 1 Corinthians 2:9.

22. See Luke 5:1-7.

23. Proverbs 13:20.

24. Psalm 1:1-3.

25. See Genesis 25:5-8; 26:1-14.

26. Napoleon Hill, *Think and Grow Rich* (New York: Hawthorn Books, 1966).

27. See Matthew 3:16.

28. Genesis 22:17a.

CHAPTER 3—MONEY AND FAITH

1. Mark 11:23.

2. Matthew 9:29 KJV.

3. See Luke 8:40-55.
4. 2 Corinthians 5:7.
5. See Ephesians 1:20; 2:6.
6. See Mark 9:23-24.
7. Proverbs 18:20a KJV.
8. John 6:5-9 paraphrased.
9. 2 Kings 4:1-7 paraphrased.
10. Genesis 1:1.
11. Genesis 1:26a KJV.
12. Genesis 1:28.
13. John 1:14.
14. Matthew 17:24-27 paraphrased.
15. See Matthew 13:3-4,19.
16. Luke 5:4b.
17. Matthew 6:19-20a.
18. Matthew 19:16-24, 27-29 paraphrased.
19. Malachi 3:10 paraphrased.
20. Genesis 28:20-22.
21. Genesis 31:10-13.
22. See Genesis 31:1-13.

Chapter 4—The Real Value of Your Mind

1. Robert Kiyosaki is an American investor, businessman, self-help author, and motivational speaker. He

is best known for his *Rich Dad, Poor Dad* series of motivational books and other material published under the Rich Dad brand.

2. Matthew 9:29 KJV.

3. See Matthew 22:37-38.

4. See Exodus 20:2-17.

5. Exodus 20:13.

6. Dr. David Oyedepo is the president of Living Faith Ministries Worldwide.

7. 1 Timothy 6:6-7,10 paraphrased.

8. Matthew 19:16-22,29 paraphrased.

9. Matthew 6:31 paraphrased.

10. See Acts 2:44-45.

11. Romans 12:2.

12. See Luke 1:26-35 paraphrased.

13. Mark 11:23.

14. Joshua 1:7a.

15. See Acts 8:26-38.

16. See Matthew 25:14–30.

17. Robert Kiyosaki and Sharon Letcher, *Rich Dad, Poor Dad* (London: Warner Books ed., 2000).

18. Proverbs 23:4a KJV.

19. See 1 Samuel 17:1-51.

20. Exodus 36:1.

CHAPTER 5—THE SPENDING PLAN

1. Matthew 25:29.
2. Habakkuk 2:1-2.
3. Luke 14:28.
4. Luke 14:31.
5. Romans 13:6-7.
6. Proverbs 21:20.
7. Exodus 20:8.
8. Ecclesiastes 5:11.
9. Proverbs 21:20b.

CHAPTER 6—BREAKING FREE FROM POVERTY

1. Acts 3:6a.
2. See Genesis 15:1-6.
3. 2 Corinthians 5:7.
4. 2 Thessalonians 3:10.
5. Genesis 8:22 paraphrased.
6. See Genesis 40:1-23; 41:1-41.
7. Proverbs 22:29.
8. Malcolm Gladwell, *The Outliers* (England: Penguin Books Limited, 2009), 38-76.
9. Genesis 41:38.
10. Ephesians 6:7-8.

11. 1 Chronicles 4:9.

12. 1 Chronicles 4:10.

13. See 1 Chronicles 4:10.

14. See Genesis 41:1-36.

15. Proverbs 21:20.

16. Philippians 4:13.

17. Philippians 4:11.

18. See Proverbs 22:7.

19. See 2 Kings 4:1-7.

20. Proverbs 30:24-25 The Message Bible.

21. See Ecclesiastes 5:11.

22. Cyril Northcote Parkinson, *Parkinson's Law* (Buccaneer Books, 1993).

23. See Numbers 8:25.

24. John 6:12 paraphrased.

25. Romans 8:14 KJV.

CHAPTER 7—STARTING A BUSINESS

1. 2 Chronicles 20:20b.

2. See 2 Kings 4:1-7.

3. See Exodus 12:35-36.

4. Genesis 30:25-27.

5. See Genesis 39:1-6.

6. 1 Corinthians 2:9-10a.

7. See Genesis 41.

8. Proverbs 22:7.

9. Zechariah 1:20-21.

10. Matthew 4:4a.

11. Acts 3:6.

12. John 8:32.

13. Deuteronomy 9:1-2.

14. Luke 14:28-29.

15. Deuteronomy 28:12.

16. Psalm 37:21.

17. Matthew 5:15.

18. Ecclesiastes 11:4 The Living Bible.

19. See Luke 10:19.

20. See Luke 11:5-10.

21. See 1 Kings 18:41-45.

22. See Joshua 6:1-20.

23. See 2 Kings 5:1-14.

24. Deuteronomy 28:1-6.

CHAPTER 8—FINANCIAL FREEDOM

1. Albert Einstein was a German-born, Swiss-American theoretical physicist, philosopher, and author widely regarded as one of the most influential and best-known scientists and intellectuals of all time. He is

often regarded as the father of modern physics, receiving the Nobel Prize in Physics in 1921.

2. Proverbs 21:5 Amplified Bible.

3. See Genesis 41:1-32.

4. Robert Allen, *Multiple Streams of Income* (New Jersey: John Wiley & Sons Inc., 2005).

5. Ecclesiastes 5:13-15 New Century Version.

6. Matthew 6:19-21.

7. Proverbs 23:4a.

8. See Genesis 14:18-20; Hebrews 7:1-10.

9. See Genesis 26:12-14.

10. Genesis 27:4.

11. Genesis 27:27-29.

12. See Genesis 27:30-38.

13. 1 Timothy 6:9.

14. See Luke 12:16-21.

15. 1 Timothy 6:10.

16. Matthew 6:24b.

17. See Hebrews 11:6.

18. 1 Timothy 6:17.

19. Malachi 3:10.

20. Mark 12:41-44.

21. Hebrews 7:7.

22. Ephesians 6:2-3.

23. 1 Samuel 9:8.

24. Acts 8:20.

25. Psalm 41:1-3.

26. Proverbs 19:17a.

27. Warren Buffett is an American investor, industrialist, and philanthropist. He is widely regarded as one of the most successful investors in the world and consistently ranked among the world's wealthiest people; net worth in September 2011 equaled $39 billion. http://www.forbes.com/profile/warren-buffett/; accessed October 3, 2011.

Contact the Author

If you would like to contact the author,
please write him at:

s.adeyemi@successpower.tv

Additional copies of this book and other book
titles from EVANGELISTA MEDIA™
and DESTINY IMAGE™ EUROPE
are available at your local bookstore.

We are adding new titles every month!

To view our complete catalog online, visit us at:
www.evangelistamedia.com

Send a request for a catalog to:

Via della Scafa, 29/14
65013 Città Sant'Angelo (Pe), ITALY
Tel. +39 085 4716623 • Fax +39 085 9090113
info@evangelistamedia.com

"Changing the World, One Book at a Time."

Are you an author?
Do you have a "today" God-given message?

CONTACT US

We will be happy to review your manuscript
for the possibility of publication:

publisher@evangelistamedia.com
http://www.evangelistamedia.com/pages/AuthorsAppForm.htm